THE ART OF DANCE COMPOSITION

The Art of Dance Composition: Writing the Body is an introduction to modern dance composition, providing clear and structured approaches to designing and defining movement that demystify the creative process.

The book introduces the concepts of creating authentic movement, processes for gathering and ordering compositional elements, and the ways in which theme, story, and design relate to bodies moving through space. It approaches the practice of composition from many avenues, including the use of digital tools such as video and video editing software, digital mapping, and motion capture, and through improvisation, sourced gestures, and inspiration from visual art, found objects, and chance methodology. Flowcharts that organize and provide a framework for making dance are included, equipping readers with a clear roadmap for creating their own work.

Filled with practical advice, this book is suitable for all aspiring choreographers.

The Art of Dance Composition: Writing the Body includes access to performance videos that demonstrate the concepts illustrated in the book. To access the videos, visit www.routledge.com/9780367424435.

Jenefer Davies is Chair of the Department of Theatre, Dance, and Film Studies and Professor of Dance at Washington and Lee University and Artistic Director of the W&L Repertory Dance Company. She is the author of *Aerial Dance: A Guide to Dance with Rope and Harness* (Routledge 2018).

THE ART OF DANCE COMPOSITION

Writing the Body

Jenefer Davies

Routledge
Taylor & Francis Group
NEW YORK AND LONDON

Designed cover image: Kevin Remington, Washington and Lee University 2016

First published 2024
by Routledge
605 Third Avenue, New York, NY 10158

and by Routledge
4 Park Square, Milton Park, Abingdon, Oxon, OX14 4RN

Routledge is an imprint of the Taylor & Francis Group, an informa business

© 2024 Taylor & Francis

The right of Jenefer Davies to be identified as author of this work has been asserted in accordance with sections 77 and 78 of the Copyright, Designs and Patents Act 1988.

All rights reserved. No part of this book may be reprinted or reproduced or utilised in any form or by any electronic, mechanical, or other means, now known or hereafter invented, including photocopying and recording, or in any information storage or retrieval system, without permission in writing from the publishers.

Trademark notice: Product or corporate names may be trademarks or registered trademarks, and are used only for identification and explanation without intent to infringe.

Library of Congress Cataloging-in-Publication Data
Names: Davies, Jenefer, author.
Title: The art of dance composition : writing the body / Jenefer Davies.
Description: New York : Routledge, 2024. | Includes bibliographical references and index.
Identifiers: LCCN 2023012647 (print) | LCCN 2023012648 (ebook) | ISBN 9780367424428 (hbk) | ISBN 9780367424435 (pbk) | ISBN 9780367824167 (ebk)
Subjects: LCSH: Choreography. | Modern dance. | Dance.
Classification: LCC GV1782.5 .D38 2024 (print) | LCC GV1782.5 (ebook) | DDC 792.8/2--dc23/eng/20230513
LC record available at https://lccn.loc.gov/2023012647
LC ebook record available at https://lccn.loc.gov/2023012648

ISBN: 978-0-367-42442-8 (hbk)
ISBN: 978-0-367-42443-5 (pbk)
ISBN: 978-0-367-82416-7 (ebk)

DOI: 10.4324/9780367824167

Typeset in Joanna
by KnowledgeWorks Global Ltd.

Access the Support Material: www.routledge.com/9780367424435

For anyone who ever wanted to create but was afraid, shy, insecure, or unsure of themselves for any reason—go get started. I believe in you.

CONTENTS

	Acknowledgments	viii
	About the author	x
	Introduction: The choreographic lens	**1**
1	**Process, an example**	**7**
2	**What is *not* dance?**	**46**
3	**Vocabulary**	**49**
4	**Authentic movement**	**58**
5	**Choreographic flowchart**	**78**
6	**(The seductive cunning of) music**	**132**
7	**Intellectual property**	**138**
8	**Advice**	**147**
9	**A conversation among artists**	**155**
	Index	177

ACKNOWLEDGMENTS

Erik Jones, my champion, my foundation, and my home

Emma Davies-Mansfield, my soul sister and forever love

Vanessa Davies for your brilliance, graciousness, and generosity

John Paulas for your creative mind and gentle heart

Liza Deck, Sandra Meythaler, and ShaLeigh Comerford: sisters in art

Dave Pfaff: digital dance partner

Sara Dotterer, Elliot Emadian, Emily Danzig, Lisa Stoiser, and Irina Koleva: dancers/artists

Kevin Remington: photographer

W&L Repertory Dance Company dancers, 2006–2023

Museums at Washington and Lee University, Lexington, Virginia

ACKNOWLEDGMENTS ix

Support for the publication of this book was provided by the Lenfest Sabbatical Endowment at Washington and Lee University

Support for the publication of this book was provided by the Class of 1956 Provost's Faculty Development Endowment at Washington and Lee University

Photographs were taken by Kevin Remington. Copyright 2006–2023. Washington and Lee University. All rights reserved.

Christen Church and Robert Briggs

I owe an extraordinary debt to the dance teachers and dance professors whose lessons are in my bones and whose wisdom still inspires me: Donna Faye Burchfield, Shelly Stewart Thompson, Paula Levine, Haruki Fujimoto, Maida Withers, Missy Augustine, and Judy Hakes

ABOUT THE AUTHOR

Credit: Courtesy of Emma Davies-Mansfield, 2020.

ABOUT THE AUTHOR

Jenefer Davies is Chair of the Department of Theatre, Dance and Film Studies and Professor of Dance at Washington and Lee University and Artistic Director of the W&L Repertory Dance Company. She received an MFA in Choreography and Performance from The George Washington University and a MALS in Dance from Hollins University. Her choreography has been commissioned by dance, opera, and theater companies and has toured to Spain, Greece, Scotland, and throughout the United States. Davies founded the contemporary modern dance company, Progeny Dance (later Davies & Dancers) that has performed at Green Space, Dixon Place, and the Ailey Citigroup Theatre in Manhattan, annually at The Center for Performance Research in Brooklyn and at the Edinburgh Fringe Festival, Ladyfest Charlotte, Richmond Dance Festival, Fort Worth Contemporary Dance Festival, and the Cucalorus Festival, among others. Her work has been supported by the Virginia Commission for the Arts; W&L Lenfest Grants, Johnson Fund, and Glenn Grants; the Treakle Foundation; and the Associated Colleges of the South Institutional grant, Mini grant, and Mellon grant, among others. She created one of the first academic programs in aerial dance in the country and her aerial dancers have performed at the Ailey Citigroup Theatre in NYC, at the Corcoran Gallery of Art in Washington DC, and from the rooftops of buildings on the Washington & Lee campus. Davies has been published in the *International Planetarian Magazine, Dance Research Journal*, the *Nu Delta Alpha Journal, and Athens Journal for Humanities and the Arts* among others, and has guest taught, lectured, choreographed, or performed at the College of William & Mary, Sweet Briar College, Hollins University, Roanoke College, Radford College, Mill Mountain Theatre, The Roanoke Symphony, Dance Forms Productions, the Southeastern Theatre Conference, United States Institute for Theatre Technology, American College Dance Association, and the American Alliance of Health, Physical Education, Recreation and Dance. She has served on the Editorial and Reviewer's Board of the *Athens Journal of Humanities and Arts* and has reviewed dance proposals for Oxford University Press. She was a fellow at the Virginia Center for Creative Arts. In 2021, she received the Outstanding Dance Research Award from the National Dance Education Organization for her work in aerial dance. Her first book *Aerial Dance: A Guide to Dance with Rope and Harness* was published by Routledge Press in 2018.

INTRODUCTION

THE CHOREOGRAPHIC LENS

Figure 0.2 Breathing Lessons.
Credit: ©Washington and Lee University 2013.

INTRODUCTION

Friends often remark that I notice and comment on details about bodies in space that go unnoticed by them. The way the banker pronates and supinates her wrist while raising it to force her bracelet to slide up her arm so she can count money without it getting in the way, or the profound hyperextension of the casher's fingers so that the pad of her fingers, not her nail extensions, hit the correct computer keys, or how the woman walking down the street has a slight hitch in her gait because she is favoring her right hip.

When questioned, I generally respond with some simple quip about how I spend my professional life watching and assessing bodies in movement. While that's true, I think it also has a lot to do with being able to read context clues, observing tiny seemingly trivial peculiarities in behavior or function, and, using anatomical landmarks, reference the issue. It's not simply that the lady favors her right hip, it's that her left hip appears to have limited range of motion and her high heels are pushing her weight forward off of her center. Combined with that, she also carries on her shoulder a big bag that is pulling down on her lumbar, is causing her abdominals to spill forward and creating lordosis. As a result, her shoulders, neck, and head alignment are compromised, throwing her knees, ankles, and feet out of alignment.

As a dance professor, choreographer, and performer, I spend most of my time every day looking at bodies moving through space and watching alignment, how the weight shifts, where the anatomical points of reference are positioned, where movement originates muscularly, where the effort originates, and how flow is achieved, among other things. These movement components are fragments of meaning that inform the whole, a collection of phrases that together create a complete thought. These fragments can be things like wrist position or angle of head that then are added to other elements like height of arm or shoulder release and presented, along with many other precise details, within the x, y, and z axes of the body. I think of them as clues. By looking for clues the body is conveying, we can make assumptions and sometimes assessments of the body as a whole. Searching for clues and expressions are also at the heart of creating, speaking, and writing about and interpreting dance works. It is within these small choices that meaning lies.

When I teach new composition students, I look for something they already understand and use that terminology to express the process of dance making. I sometimes use the analogy of essay writing; words become phrases that grow into sentences and then paragraphs. A paragraph has a topic sentence and then supporting sentences that contain explanations or elaborations. There may be an introduction that alludes to something to be revealed later or a conclusion that summarizes or makes a final comment. If you're dealing with emotions or story, there may be rising action that is born of conflict or an argument that is made, a climax where the problem or crisis reaches its peak, sometimes there is an aftermath of the climax, and maybe, if the piece calls for it, a resolution.

Although the process of writing is complex, moving back and forth between thoughts, sentences, and paragraphs in a recursive way, most students in my experience haven't been taught or don't understand this process. Therefore, using writing as an example for choreographic purposes is flawed in that it causes the students to presuppose a linear structure to dance composition. To them, it assumes a definitive answer or solution waiting at the end of the path if only each step is properly executed. It assumes a single point of view. The concept of editing, however, may be more relevant. The writer reviews and edits each paragraph in and of itself and then again as a group of paragraphs and again as a paper. Endings may bring about changes in the beginning, and the completed work may diverge from the original intention that inspired its writing. Although the thematic material or structure of the dance may not follow a linear path, the piece itself has a beginning, middle, and end so can be modeled that way. This enables one to speak about, dissect, and edit the work.

Another, perhaps more relevant, analogy I sometimes use is painting; painting requires consideration of hue, value, and saturation. For each area of the painting, these considerations must be deliberated upon and chosen based upon the artist's story, theme, or idea. Once chosen, the artists' tools for communication grow to include the focal point, the rules of thirds, the horizon line, rhythm, balance, movement, for example. These elements either refer back to previous marks or forge ahead with related or new marks. Each mark broadens the painting and requires further choices. Marks become shapes that grow into images and slowly begin to fill the canvas. Problems arise and are either dealt with within the context of the painting or covered over, hidden, and repainted. Choices create layers and depths, both literal and metaphorical. Within the thematic material of the subject, some painter's tools are used, and others are forgotten. What the painter says and how they choose to say it is revealed through dabs, strokes, shapes, pressure, and line, among other things. Elements are reviewed, edited, changed, and reviewed again both, at a small scale each time new paint is applied and, at a large scale, within the painting as a whole in a relentless circle until the artist chooses to be finished.

This painting metaphor appeals to me more so than the essay writing metaphor because its very structure is undefined. Its starting place isn't one inch from the left of the page with the expectation that it will proceed from left to right until the page break. A painting can begin anywhere on the canvas and move in any direction. Changing the analogy to sculpting allows us to add a three-dimensional quality as well. This makes sense to my choreographer's brain because this is how I work.

I've found over the years, though, that young choreographers relate to the writing example because they've had years of experience practicing and perfecting that particular model in traditional classrooms. With these students, my aim is to gently, over time, guide them from the essay writing example to one of poetry so they can begin to create not only linear constructions but also compositions whose words move around on the page in any way the author wishes. The transition is smooth because writing and poetry share an alphabet and vocabulary and are a verbal means of expression. But poetry offers the freedom to move the words around the page with impunity, to use text to make images, and to adhere to or imagine their own punctuation and spelling. It's my hope that, eventually, the free form nature of poetry that can break the conventions of grammar will encourage the students to work less linearly and more abstractly.

While sorting through my copious files pertaining to my piece m(other), I read through old faculty activity reports, grant applications, choreographic notes, and emails with producers and presenters. I reviewed old videos from rehearsals and pages and pages of choreographic and

INTRODUCTION 5

feedback notes. Through this organizational process, I learned something interesting about the way I work that I hadn't previously known. It may be that my life is so jam packed with work, projects, side projects, and side-side projects that I never had the time to pause. It may also be a forest/tree thing. To draw parallels between life and work, I needed the distance of not 10 feet and a single day but a 1000 feet and three years. Or maybe (although I'd hate it if it were true) I'm not contemplative enough (or patient enough?) and tend to push on to the next idea as soon as I've burned through a previous project, seeking a new spark to ignite my interests.

But looking back, I began to see connections between things. The associations are so evident when you have four or five years of hindsight and the intellectual and kinesthetic knowledge that comes from experiencing them. By *experiencing*, I mean delving deep; reading, writing, researching, abstracting, moving, creating, editing, repeating, revising, and originating thematic material. Then, taking that thematic material and looking at it through a lens, backwards, upside down and inverted. Gathering what is left and looking at it again to enhance, clarify, delve deeper, stretch, obscure, or throw away. Repeating this process for every step, every phase, every idea. Repeating this process within ideas, within steps, within concepts. It's easy to get caught in the minutiae because, really, minutiae is its essence. Precise details are part of what is created, gathered, organized, and attached and, eventually, create phrases. Those phrases are looked at, grouped, moved about, and gathered to make the crux of an idea. These ideas grow into a structure that is the beginnings of communication. This process strikes at the heart of me personally and comprises a large part of who I am as a choreographer.

Since gathering and perusing all my old materials, I have noticed that because I created this piece over the course of three years or more, the unrelated (or so I thought at the time) projects that I was working on before and in tandem with this choreographic work fed into and informed it. Having said this, it really doesn't sound like a major revelation, I suppose. It makes sense that, although we are multifaceted humans, we also have interests of focus and issues that are meaningful in special ways. I seem drawn over and over again to exploring the inherent strength of women. I've displayed this research through dances

6 INTRODUCTION

rife with irony, through comedy, by autobiographical work, and as hyper abstracted pieces. So, it does seem plausible that my work fits together. I suppose that what's interesting to me is that I thought I was working on independent projects made specifically for festivals or concerts or artists. But it seems that maybe what I was really doing was telling my story, via a serpentine path without context or time frame, one dance at a time.

I named this book *Writing the Body* not solely because the Greek roots for "choreograph" is *dance* and *writing*. I also love the concept of the body being a storyteller, a truth teller, a communicative vessel, and the idea that by arranging shape, time, effort, and design, we can write a story told through the human form. While originally the term "choreographer" referred to the person who documented steps and phrases, by the nineteenth century, the meaning evolved and the term for that activity shifted to "dance notator," while choreographer came to mean the person who engages in the artistic practice of organizing movement in time and space. Shapemaking, orientation, stage balance, methods of shifting between shapes, ways of arranging bodies, creating negative space between bodies, and countless other approaches to design mean that the writer of the body has a massive toolbox from which to choose. It's the use and organization of these tools that makes dance, (for the purposes of this book specifically, modern dance), nimble, ever-changing, dynamic, and exciting.

A personal note as you proceed through this book; I am a female-identifying person, and so I use words like "women" and concepts like the "suffering and demoralizing of women" with the understanding that these words and concepts can apply to people born as women and people who identify as women. It's my hope that weaving my personal story into the fabric of this book as a way to illuminate, comment on, and connect to my life as a choreographer will highlight the interconnectedness of art and life and be an inclusive experience. Further, I use she, he, and their/they/them interchangeably throughout this book. This is also intentional because, while some of my thematic material pertains specifically to issues involving women and woman identifying individuals, I want the content of this book to be available, applicable, and inviting to anyone who is interested in creating art through movement.

1
PROCESS, AN EXAMPLE

Figure 1.1 Anagrammed.
Credit: ©Washington and Lee University, 2019.

Sometimes, the best way to discuss a subject as intangible as dance with new choreography students is through reverse engineering. By this I mean that, for educational purposes, I sometimes like to begin with the final product and look to see how we arrived there. Past experience setting the work, rehearsal and performance video, choreographic notes, etc. give one the opportunity to use the finished product as a model. It is something we can look at, listen to, and rewind and fast forward for multiple viewings, which gives us something to discuss.

The contrasting nature of the foundational elements within musical theater choreography and concert dance choreography serves as an interesting example. In a typical musical, there is generally a score and a story or a theme. These elements serve as a frame upon which you can build a dance. You have a starting place from which to begin. Concert dance is challenging because you're building something from nothing. There is no pre-existing story or score, nothing in which to ground the work. This can be scary. It's like looking at a blank page knowing you have to write an essay about a topic of your choice. There seem to be limitless possibilities. Standing in an empty studio with the directive to create can be similarly daunting.

By working backward, we first see the finished product and then all the steps that lead there. A discussion can ensue based on existing movement, confirmed thematic material, and bodies in space. Gone is the added stress of figuring out where to begin and how to talk about the work because it's already there. This process of reverse engineering is a gentle first step for new composers. Hopefully, if I've done my job right, students will come to understand over time that the freedom that comes from choreographing dance isn't scary, it's liberating. It's an exciting blank canvas, not a gaping hole. But for those who are still hesitant, later in the book I discuss in-depth ways in which you can set your own boundaries or create a custom framework for yourself, if you wish.

I used the mechanism of reverse engineering here to tell a personal story of the process. In the course of writing this chapter, I began with the final version of a piece of choreography and traced it backward through all of its iterations to what inspired it, where the inspiration originated, and the underpinning of the origin story. After I had rediscovered that original inspiration, then for the purposes of storytelling, I took the choreography-in-reverse notes that I had written for myself and arranged them in chronological order.

A work of choreography may require years of development to reach full fruition. In laying out its history and the piece's many iterations, I will show how it was influenced and grew over that span of time by things occurring elsewhere in my life. This story will highlight the interconnectedness of life and art and how they support and influence each other. Above all, this account is about the process: how the dance evolved from a philosophical idea twenty years ago, what prompted the stages of evolution, and the development of the dance work over the course of four years. I will show that over the course of almost four years, it changed casts, music, length, and titles. It was expounded upon, edited, grew, and deepened. The core, however, remained the same. It has always been a dance/theater piece; by that, I mean a piece that incorporates dance, spoken word, acting, storytelling, sets, props. It leaned more heavily toward the storytelling direction at some points and more toward abstraction at others. Student dancers informed some choices, and their work and contributions informed certain sections.

The growth and changes that this piece went through would not have been possible if it hadn't had multiple performances, viewings, and casts throughout its development. Seeing a piece through the eyes of the audience is much different than seeing through a rehearsal lens. Each audience member brings their history, experiences, and views of themselves and the world to the theater. Their lenses perceive my work through their biases and interpret it with no insight into my artistic intent. This means that, generally, their perceptions of my work are as varied as their life experiences. While audience responses don't dictate future choices I make, I am grateful for feedback as that information helps me see the work from new viewpoints, which sometimes becomes part of my future creative process. In the same way, having multiple and varied casts informs my process as I observe how they interpret and process my material. Throughout its incarnations, this work was shown at Dixon Place in New York City, NY; the Center for Performance Research in Brooklyn, NY; the Ailey Citibank Theatre in Manhattan, NY; the Taubman Museum of Art in Roanoke, VA; and multiple times at both the Johnson and Keller Stages in the Lenfest Center for the Arts at the college where I teach.

What follows is a detailed account of one choreographic work.

Without knowing or planning it, the work on this piece began over twenty years ago when I wrote an article that questioned if modern dance was a feminine aesthetic. I was interested in the fact that the pioneers of modern dance were mostly women and fascinated by the idea of them fashioning this new way of moving on their womanly bodies. I wondered how using a woman's body as the landscape for creating and performing dance could alter movement. Would it be gentler? More powerful? With softer or more angled shapes? Less or more virtuosic? Would nuance play a role? Similarly, I wondered if a dance form that was based upon and made for women would speak more clearly to woman dancers, choreographers, and audiences who identify as women. Does the open, roundness of female pelvises contribute to the shape of torso movement? How does having breasts alter balance or alignment? Do people with female-identified bodies move differently because of them? Further, in what ways does a feminist foundation contribute to being a human who identifies as a female dancer? A female choreographer? Does it contribute to thematic material? To performance expectations? To production values? While no one woman is like another, does it follow that the shape and form of dance made for a woman's body could look like a male version of such? Can a man dance a woman's form? Clearly, they can and have done so for over a hundred years. But the philosophical questions remained with me. The young dancer in me wanted modern to be for me, special to women, anatomically kindred, unique among dance forms.

This question and the need to find a home for my body and practice, while dormant temporarily in terms of active research, was on my mind as I watched my body change and adapt to my own pregnancy. During that time, I was serving as the artistic and executive director for a dance company and school, teaching daily, and adjuncting at two colleges. I watched in wonder as typical pregnancy-related changes happened to my body but was truly fascinated by what was to me unexpected. At the time, an interesting change to me was the way in which the bones in my pelvis seemed to open due to the softening of the pelvic ligaments.

I noticed that my pelvis became more elastic, and for the first time ever, when sitting on the floor with my legs together and straight out in front of me, I could touch my nose to my knees and lay my entire torso on my legs (until my belly got too big). As someone who struggled somewhat with flexibility as a young dancer, it was so exciting. It felt like magic. Moving from my center became an interesting challenge as my center shifted, and because I was also choreographing for a professional theater, I learned quickly when I had to hold on to my belly in order to move in certain ways. For me, the actual act of giving birth was simple and fast. I think it was probably just luck and/or genetics but it definitely didn't hurt that I had such a deep knowledge of my body, an internal kinesthetic and proprioceptive understanding, and a clear mind/body communication that was already in place.

During the first few years of my daughter's life, through research and experimentation, I became more and more aware that a connection between modern dance, feminism, and mothering exists. Of course, history is there to be read and watched, and multiple articles and papers have been written on the topic, but the search became something private for me. I craved a personal connection in which all three of these facets existed, informing and playing off of one another. I realized only later that much of the choreography I created and presented during this time was thematically and kinesthetically linked to this idea. The works dealt with powerful dancers working low to the floor, sliding, running, stomping with stifled power. The pieces were devised with dynamic movement and flailing appendages, deep resonating rhythms, and almost primal strength. Looking back on that body of work in its entirety, I can see that my search gave birth to my desire to demonstrate and affirm the power of women. It became a recurring theme in my work and still is.

In 2013, I received funding from my university to travel to the West Coast with the goal of interviewing professional ballet and modern dancers from large companies who have had babies and then returned to performing. In addition to my long-standing interest in the intersectionality of modern dance, feminism, and mothering, I became interested in particular in the changing emotional and psychological connections dancers have with their bodies during and after pregnancy, the physical knowledge of the dancer versus body knowledge that is only obtainable through the act of pregnancy and childbirth, and whether the intimate connection between the dancer and her body complicates or augments the pregnancy. I pondered whether the transformations of pregnancy were more poignant for a dancer, as opposed to a woman who doesn't dance, with the idea that the dancer lives more acutely inside her body. I wondered what it means that a dancer chooses to have a baby at all, given that her body is the tool of her trade. The condition of a dancer's body defines the way she functions professionally, and her achievements are measured by physical performance. I questioned the presence of psychological and emotional shifts from artist to mother and back again.

This time spent with professional dancers was illuminating and brought about further questions concerning differing views I perceived in the philosophies of mothering and performance between choreographers and performers and between ballet and modern dancers. Many, if not all, of the people I interviewed expressed the sentiment that the concept of informed movement stemming from a childbearing experience was something that they hadn't previously considered. It was clear that some dancers looked upon their bodies as instruments of work, like a computer or fax machine that does a job. Their home life was very separate, and they found no connection between these experiences. Yet others regaled me with personal *bodystories* and spoke of a new awareness that improved the relationship between their bodies and their dance technique. Some even used the experience thematically in their work and drew upon their history when making new work.

Interested in expanding upon what I learned from the West Coast interviews, the next year I decided to conduct interviews with professional dancers in New York City. This allowed me to broaden my research geographically, include a greater number of dancers in my study, and create more directed questions. I used my professional and academic contacts to create a list of dancers who either took time off from dancing to have a child and later returned to work or quit dancing professionally upon becoming pregnant but stayed in the field through teaching and/ or amateur performance. I spent quite a bit of time creating a detailed questionnaire both as an exercise for myself to clarify the subject matter and in preparation for scheduling interviews.

I sought to determine if there are differences in their experiences based on the style of dance that the woman performed or was trained in, if there were differences between women who danced for a company or danced as independent artists, and those who are teaching artists as opposed to performing artists. These questions were specifically targeted to garner a wide range of perspectives on mothering bodies from the professional dance world. I discussed these topics in private meetings and allowed the conversation to develop organically based on the individual and her experiences. I recorded the stories from dancers that included body education, challenges in work and life, alterations to views on performance and mothering, physical, emotional, and psychological shifts, and adjustment. I investigated whether these dancers learned new things about their bodies through pregnancy and childbirth that are applicable to their professional lives, whether they overcame challenges when reentering the field, and if childbirth informed their performance, movement quality, or thematic material.

I was able to interview both ballet and modern dancers and compare and contrast their responses with the body knowledge instilled in them through their specific dance form. For example, generally, modern dancers are taught as part of their practice to listen to their bodies, to open lines of communication, to exchange information, and to make choices based on what their bodies are telling them. I wonder then, does this cause them to be more open to the changes that their bodies are going through during pregnancy? Compared to ballet dancers, are modern dancers more readily able to rejoin the world of professional modern dance due to its less stringent aesthetic demands? How do the dancers adjust the way they move or their alignment or center of weight to compensate for changes in their anatomy? If a dancer has been taught to only replicate an image or a shape but not to feel the shape deeply, will that lead to less connection to the birthing process? Will she struggle more with the physical changes? Does the body-mind connection with respect to movement have any bearing on birthing? We know, for example, that the musculoskeletal effects of pregnancy include the separating of the pubic bones and shifting of the pelvic alignment. I was interested in how this physical change, which is so basic and happens to every woman who is able and wishes to bear a child, affects women whose bodies are not only their livelihood but with which they have the most intimate of connections.

Although the original plan for the summer portion of this project was organized and detailed, I (ironically) neglected to take into consideration the realities of being a professional dancer and mother living and working in New York City. The incredibly hectic schedules of the dancer/mothers and their lack of time altered my plans for the research slightly. Their schedules and availability were so divergent that in order to conduct all of my interviews, I would have had to either make fifteen to twenty trips to New York City or stay locally in NYC for a month or more. As neither of these options was reasonable given my distance from NYC, instead of traveling to interview them face-to-face, I corresponded with them via email and communication by telephone. Although I felt this was a less intimate way of communicating about a very personal subject, my options were limited. Similarly, many of the interviewees were new mothers, and although they expressed deep interest in the subject as well as the outcomes of my research, some of them ended up opting out of even the long-distance interview citing lack of time. Due to this, the number of mother/dancers whom I was able to connect with was smaller than I wished. However, those whom I did interview were very open and forthcoming with their experiences, and my data ended up being quite deep and layered.

As I assessed my data, which inevitably lead to more questions and deeper thought, I was also working on a new piece of choreography. I wanted to creatively express my thoughts about these interviews and where I was in my study of the intersection of mothering and modern dance. Because that year we planned to perform in a small black box theater, the intimacy of the space fits perfectly with the intimacy of my subject. To express where my thoughts and research lay, I titled the concert *The Beauty Project*. This theme spoke to me and seemed a perfect avenue for linking my notes on mothering with images of mothers' bodies and raising the question of how beauty can be found in scarring, stretch marks, and stitches.

I began by sending out a blast email and posting an ad on our university campus email system. I indicated that I was looking for mothers who would be willing to allow me to photograph the artifacts of childbirth.

I explained that I'd be happy to photograph whatever part of their body they'd like to share and that there would be no nudity requirement if that concerned them. I waited but got no response. Knowing the pressures involving body image and motherhood in general that women face, I wondered if the lack of response was a result of embarrassment. I sent out a second plea and expounded upon the privacy angle, saying I'd be happy to photograph them close up so there would be no identifying features in the finished project. Nothing. Crickets.

To this day, I'm not sure why no one was interested. I guess it could have been because I was new to the faculty and so therefore an unknown quantity. I pondered but hoped it was not that the women are ashamed about the marks made from pregnancy and childbirth. Or even still, it could have been quite simple; they had children and were working full time and therefore had no time to spare. Delving into the *whys* of this situation wasn't my aim, so I moved on. I'd still very much like to finish (well, start) this project.

Acquiescence

Figure 1.2 Acquiescence.
Credit: ©Washington and Lee University, 2010.

PROCESS, AN EXAMPLE

Since I didn't have models, I researched images and chose ones that I felt were beautiful but probably didn't fit the typical definition of beauty. Armed with these images, I began an exploration of movement that was low, deep, powerful, and pulsating. I wanted to express the innate power of women and the driving forces within them that enable them to withstand pain, that empower them to take on this awesome responsibility, as well as the power of the body to bend, flex, and change as necessary to create new life. As with most of my work, I start with thematic intent, and that led to the movement. The movement is constructed, edited, discarded, added to, amplified, turned on its head, reversed, revised, revised, and revised. The words became phrases and then language and it began to speak for me. It revealed hidden power in an outwardly facing softness: contemplation while screaming, thoughtfulness while flailing. The inward storm juxtaposed against the outward calm began to emerge.

When setting work on students (or really any situation that isn't working with professional dancers), sometimes the cast dictates some of the choices I make. Such was the case with this piece. Nearly always, I find that having fewer options available, rather than detracting from a piece, actually helps shape it in unintended but unfailingly interesting ways. Because I was working with new dancers, I added a shapemaking portion to the piece, one in which dancers used images as inspiration. I asked them to interpret images that were projected onto a screen on stage, and then I edited, arranged, and set them. I chose to use images of saints and angels from stained glass windows because I felt they captured a traditional definition of beauty primarily due to the shape and form of the artists' interpretation of the body but also due to the artists' view of their angelic state of grace. I felt they would be nicely juxtaposed against a less accepted definition of beauty in the torn skin and the stapled bellies of the pregnancy and birth photos. I also liked the otherworldly angelic quality of the church windows superimposed on the deep, abrading power of the movement style.

The juxtaposition of the saintly and the vulgar was interesting to me. I questioned if beauty might be an element of both. I wondered what it meant to give consent without words and what implied agreement meant. I pondered regret in terms of career or family and the fact that, in many cases, so many of these weighty issues become the sole responsibility of the woman. She is at once powerful and powerless, leader and oppressed, supported and alone. These thoughts were reverberating around in my head when I came across a beautiful piece of writing composed by Marie Howe, the state poet of New York. Her poem is entitled "Annunciation." A few lines, abstracted here, struck me as relating to my work:

> I know it is—and that if once it hailed me
> it ever does—
> And so it is myself I want to turn in that direction.[1]

Being able to determine your own destiny is power. Being given a choice is powerful. Heeding the call, which appears to be of import in the poem, was secondary to my interests at that point. Acquiescence is part of the story, but I wondered if maybe it wasn't the most powerful part. Maybe it's the result of it. This led me to incorporate this poem into my piece. I had the dancer speak it so that the element of humanity was present in the words. Specifically, for this dance, the humanity of a woman is so important, a woman who is choosing to turn in a direction. I loved the physicality of that. It's a choice she makes and then she grounds that decision in the physical.

While working on these various sections of the piece, I felt the need to, at times, separate the conflicting juxtapositions visually. I wanted to elevate some portions of the movement but have the flexibility to move them around. Part of this was practical because the stage space was not only small but also flat with a raked audience. The scope of the choreography and the design of the piece needed height somewhere, and I liked the idea of a raised platform that could lock to the floor but also could be moved when needed. Our production team built a black square that was about six feet across and a foot or so off the ground. We chose black so that it would recede from the audience's vision, a square shape so that it had hard edges and points that referenced pain, but built it on air castors so that it appeared to float.

Again, I was interested in an association, a correlation between disparate elements. I used it quietly to raise the dancers who were shapemaking. I used its speed to carry dancers from place to place. It rolled when needed and could be clamped down when not. It provided another layer of meaning, a visual element, and also a conveyance. During the poem mentioned above, I directed to stagehands to rotate the platform she was standing on while she spoke the words. It gave the illusion that she chose to physically move but was imbued with the power to have others move her in a way that suited her needs. Throughout the dance, I used its turning capabilities to reference a clock, time passing, the cyclical nature of women and fertility, and, at the end of the dance, a record spinning that is abruptly stopped with just a finger.

When I create work, I often layer the music onto the choreography after the piece is set. Music is powerful. If a choreographer is not careful, music can dictate the flow, feel, and composition of the dance. I wanted the dance to speak for itself, so I created the movement phrases and then later—much later—put music on top of the piece. As so often happens, there were moments in performance where it looked as if the dance had been deliberately set to the music. There were few instances of coming together. Honestly, those moments were so lovely, so fleeting that I probably couldn't have created them on purpose if I intended to.

These occasions, when the dancing and the music appeared to match and reinforce their connection, were serendipitous, lovely artistic partners. I chose "Era Più Calmo?," "Piangea Cantando," and "Ave Maria" from Act 4 of Verdi's *Otello* as the first piece and followed it up with "Missed Me" by the Dresden Dolls. The high soprano voice of Renee Fleming was a stark contrast to the Dresden Dolls' self-described "Brechtian punk cabaret" style music and their frank, possibly offensive lyrics, "If you kiss me, mister, you must think I'm pretty, and if you think so, mister, you must want to f* me, if you f* me mister, it must mean you love me."

It hurts my choreographer's eye and sensibility to look back nine years and watch this piece. I see all the things I could have done better and

PROCESS, AN EXAMPLE   19

wonder how I could possibly have made some of those choices. I see heavy-handedness with the juxtaposition of music types, lack of grace in the video/music collaboration, and clunky phrases of movement that I would later hack up and reorient for inclusion in a new, better way. At times, I beat the audience over the head with the theme, and other times it seems just a mishmash of running from one place to another, or worse, the use of choreographic repetition that was so egregious it makes you want to tear out your eyeballs. (Hyperbole is my way of expressing my frustration.)

Like most choreographers, I assume, when I am ready to show my work in a concert setting, it's not that I feel it's finished, it's just that it's time to show the piece. I think of opening night as the day in which I show the work in progress. I keep working through production week, and I continue on after the last show to edit, change, and rehearse until the opening night of the next concert. Watching the piece performed through the eyes of the audience was beneficial because it helped me to back up, away from the details, and see the piece from a sweeping view, as if from the top of a mountain. It's very helpful because, at that moment, I'm not looking for the angle of the leg or the positioning of the head, I'm looking for motif, for design, for overarching story. It enables me to see the artwork, not the strokes, to see the mystery, not the clues. It's also why I keep working on the piece long after the show has closed. Viewing your own choreography from the point of view of the audience yields valuable information.

Well, here it is in all its (not so much) glory. I would like to add a small note here to say that my criticism of this piece concerns my composition only. I was then and still am proud of the student dancers in this piece. When I watch this, I see them reaching for technique and phrasing that challenges them. I see them pushing themselves in new and uncomfortable ways, and I love that. Choreographers clearly make demands on their dancers to move in specific ways. Many times, student dancers are asked to move in ways they've never previously experienced. I am grateful that they trust me as a choreographer and accept what I give them with an open and willing heart. I see many things in this piece that I will later correct, but the dancers aren't one of them.

VIDEO REFERENCE 1.1

Acquiescence

The title of this dance was born out of my response to the interviews with the dancer/mothers, my own ever-growing recognition of what motherhood was during the early years of my daughter's life, and the movement I was making for this piece. Mothering is such a profound choice. It seems to me that it's one of the few life choices that we take on without really knowing what we're getting into. I remember leaving the hospital with my one-day-old baby and saying to my husband, "I feel like I should've had to study for years and pass extensive oral and written tests before being allowed to leave with this tiny girl." We can read books and babysit children but the bodily changes, powerful physical, emotional, and psychological connection is not something one can truly know without experiencing it.

The words of the many interviews I did with dancer/mothers reminded me of the uncertainly I felt when I left the hospital. Their choice wasn't solely whether to have a baby and the many changes and adaptations inherent in that choice but also whether to put their careers on the line temporarily or even permanently. The choice involved allowing their bodies to change and gambling on whether they could rebound to reclaim the position they'd previously occupied or if they'd have to fight to get roles and find their way back professionally.

To be sure, there are mothers who jump into motherhood with joy, and I applaud them. There are also those for whom motherhood is a dream that can never be fulfilled, which is profoundly sad. However, I chose the word acquiescence because it implies consent through silence. Agreement to be sure but one that has elements of fear, of the unknown. The word felt like permission with hesitancy. Not that a baby isn't wanted, because it surely is, but because there were so many potentially life-changing unknowns above and beyond those that come with the child. I chose this title because it spoke to me personally and seemed to fit the many women that I interviewed.

The B Side

Figure 1.3 The B-Side.
Credit: ©Washington and Lee University, 2017.

An invitation, which at the time seemed to be unrelated, put me on track to edit, expand, and reinvent this work. A few months after the performance, a fellow artist invited me to create something small for inclusion in a performance at the Taubman Museum of Art in Roanoke, VA. For this piece, I wanted to work with two student dancers in particular. I chose them because they are lovely dancers and, additionally, I felt that they were ready for expanded performing roles. It seemed as though they were considering incorporating dance into their lives after college, so I felt these sorts of experiences and connections could serve them well. So, from day one, I knew I was making a duet. Because the subject matter I'd been dealing with all year was heavy, I felt compelled to create something light and straightforward. This ended up being a fortuitous development because, ultimately, I not only used this piece as one element in the ongoing large piece, but its structure and nature pushed me into a new direction for the overall work.

The parameters I set for myself for this little duet was to use a stereotypical boy/girl relationship in all of its binary 1950s squeaky-clean connotations, include music that supports this image and costumes/lighting that underscores it, but use choreography to say something different. In only three minutes, my goal was to share weight, share space, incorporate woman lifting man, incorporate woman leading man, expose strength in both parties, and create an egalitarian duet. Of course, this is nothing groundbreaking. Plenty of choreographers have addressed these issues and produced much more important work than this. For me, it was a fun, little experiment where I challenged myself to make everything except the choreography say one thing and the choreography say the opposite.

VIDEO REFERENCE 1.2

The B-Side

This piece was also performed a little later that summer at the Ailey Citibank Theatre in Manhattan. This performance had a very different audience, and the reception also contrasted. It's hard to say why one audience feels something deeper than others. I can't predict why the first small, rural community received it in a polite manner, clapping conservatively, while the city audience was raucous. There are too many variables to pinpoint a single reason for such dissimilar receptions, but it's interesting, nonetheless. I named this piece *The B-Side*, which referenced seven-inch vinyl records that contained singles. The B-side of the record was, generally, the side that doesn't contain the hit song. The title references the woman in that she doesn't receive the attention, approval, or respect from society or her partner. But in the dance, she takes it.

As I sat through rehearsals and performances, I began to see how, although outwardly completely different, the piece related to themes in *Acquiescence*. It dealt with power structures and imbalances, and sexism, and its structure was formed through the contrast of the female and male figures performing the dance roles traditionally assigned to each other. Clearly, I wasn't finished telling my story.

The 25th of March

Figure 1.4 The 25th of March.
Credit: ©Washington and Lee University 2015.

As my semester-long sabbatical began, I had time to look deeply at the intersection of mothering, feminism, and beauty and, because I had worked with Marie Howe's poem and set part of the original piece to the *Ave Maria* from Act 4 of Verdi's *Otello*, I felt myself pondering the Christian story of the Annunciation. I set a goal for my leave to create a substantial piece of choreography that expressed an abstraction of the Annunciation story in a theatrical dance format and from a feminist perspective.

To create this format, I knew that I wanted to include visual art, poetry, music, and storytelling. I spent time online with classical and modern interpretations of the subject matter. I spent time studying Roman Catholic Marian art, Eastern Orthodox icons, and late Medieval and early Renaissance works that dealt with the subject. Of particular interest because of its age was the oldest known fresco of the Annunciation, dating back to the second century. Equally challenging and engaging were works by contemporary artist John Collier, whose depiction brings

PROCESS, AN EXAMPLE

ancient iconography to modern-day suburbia, and artist Henry Ossawa Tanner, who mimics the placement and positioning of Mary found in Fra Angelico's famous painting of the Annunciation yet eschews the Renaissance master's opulent setting in favor of simple peasants' clothes and modest surroundings.

Concurrent to that line of research, which I felt depicted an idealized version of "woman" as seen through a male lens, I began looking for more images of mothering that depicted the reality of the body of the woman during pregnancy and after giving birth. Photos of new mothers with stretch marks, staples, and stitches were plentiful on the internet, and most often accompanied personal narration that told a story for each body scar. Similar to my earlier work, I wished to use both sets of images, projected onto a fifteen-foot-wide screen at various times throughout the dance piece.

I went back to the beautiful piece of writing entitled "Annunciation," composed by Marie Howe, chancellor of the Academy of American Poets and poet laureate of New York State:

> *Even if I don't see it again—nor ever feel it*
> *I know it is—and that if once it hailed me*
> *it ever does—*
> *And so it is myself I want to turn in that direction*
> *not as towards a place, but it was a tilting*
> *within myself,*
> *as one turns a mirror to flash the light to where*
> *it isn't—I was blinded like that—and swam*
> *in what shone at me*
> *only able to endure it by being no one and so*
> *specifically myself I thought I'd die*
> *from being loved like that.*[2]

I discovered an unexpected intimacy in this familiar story. I felt there was something special about the idea of a woman being herself and being acknowledged for her uniqueness. I loved the idea of swimming in love as if it were a tangible substance, and the concept of being "no one" yet revered for being oneself. I knew that this poem would play a very important role in this piece.

PROCESS, AN EXAMPLE   25

My study of music for the work occurred at a time when I was debating, in general, the use of a collection of music of a particular style or artist within one piece. I had just seen Trey McIntyre's *Mercury Half Life*, which pays homage to Queen by using well over thirty minutes of famous musical works by the band. I had also read about Doug Elkin's *M(oor)town Redux*, a retelling of Othello using only Motown music. After creating *The B-Side*, I'd been contemplating using music from the 1950s both for the symmetry of its rhythms and for its thematic contradictions. The squeaky-clean image of beach babies and poodle skirts contrasted well with the gritty underbelly of that era's struggles with racial inequality and political strife and, for my purposes, sexism, marginalization, and the inequality of women. I wanted the music to reflect the idealist version of women in art and story, which I then used to explore the realities of difficult decisions regarding childbirth, the bodily changes in the act itself, and the realities of womanhood. I wanted the music and thematic material to be like a thin veneer of fictitious superficiality layered over a deep and meaningful chasm of reality. I felt this was fertile ground for creativity.

I studied Biblical accounts of the Annunciation, as well as reactions to them from scholars and theologians—specifically those written from feminist viewpoints. This research helped to shape the piece, and I decided to create specific portions of the dance that related to *agape*, *eros*, and *philos*, all interpretations of the concept of love. Expounding on love and relationships in a general sense gave the piece an overall shape and helped to direct the more feminist aspects of my point of view. My performance piece began to take shape and included story, poetry, visual images, biblical research, and music.

It was important that the stage design reflect the thematic material of the piece that was more extensive than just a set or prop pieces. I wanted projected images to be the "set" and for them to be so large that they played a central role in the story. After conferring with designers, we chose to first create as much space as possible. We pulled out all of the legs, took away the curtains that usually mask the lights and all of the soft goods, and removed the cyclorama to reveal the shop garage door and cinderblock walls. The space was huge with hard edges and corners. The architecture of the space was evident as were the dancers. By removing the curtains that hid the stage machinery, we revealed the backstage. There was no longer stage space that hid corners for storage, paths for performer crossovers, and tech and dressing areas. Not only did this create room to fully project into the space, but the space was so vast that even with the entire cast of thirteen dancers on stage, they were diminutive. The stage space gave us the opportunity to include other smaller set pieces to fly or roll in when needed while still keeping the space open for projections.

Veering away from the heavy-handed and emotionally weighted previous work, I wanted to imbue this piece with a bit of levity between its more serious moments. I thought it would be fun to reimagine the character of the Archangel Gabriel, who in biblical stories was tasked with visiting Mary bearing the news of the impeding birth of Jesus. I portrayed this character via the most likely of messengers, a United Parcel Service (UPS) carrier.

I opened the dance with people walking purposefully, as if on a street, and cast a student actor as the UPS man. He was costumed as you might expect, brown hat, brown shirt, and brown shorts. I used spoken word to relay that he had a package and was looking for someone, but couldn't find her. His appearance was a recurring one throughout the piece to thread together the various parts. I liked the idea of him having to find the perfect person for the package. I set up a scenario wherein there was no name on the package, and he didn't know who the recipient was. No one could take it except the one for whom it was meant, and only she knew who she was. This gave him purpose throughout the piece.

As the introduction progressed, one woman organically flowed out of the maelstrom of people to walk alone onstage. As this transition happened, a frame flew in from upstage. The frame was about twenty-five feet across, half-filled the proscenium opening, and was constructed to look like shards of wood. I chose this design feature to reflect, through abstraction, the crown of thorns, the eventual end of the human life of Jesus. The frame, throughout this entire work, served as a portal through which people can pass but also (with the aid of an accompanying screen) upon which images would be projected. It helped to define a place and created a synthesis between the visual and human characters which was missing in the first iteration of this dance.

The second section of the dance began as one dancer entered into the space from inside the frame and joined the single woman on stage. As a means of introduction of the dance cast to the audience, I challenged myself to play with accumulation. I started with two dancers and anytime the movement phrases ended near the edge of the stage or at the corner, a few dancers joined, and the group seemingly multiplied out of thin air. In order to facilitate this movement, my second self-imposed challenge was to work with only a few phrases and create the dance based on reorganizing and reorienting those specific vocabularies. The initial phraseology was repeated, parts of it were reversed, the order was mixed up, factions of small groups split off to begin the phrase again but began the repeat from the middle of the original phrase, and some factions rejoined the group but changed their facing from the original or switched their timing. At the closing notes of the piece (set to "Johnny B Goode" by Chuck Berry), twelve dancers rushed off stage together as one single dancer walked through the center of the melee in the opposite direction. At the same time, a screen lowered, and the lights faded slowly until all that was left was a single side light illuminating the dancer.

In the next section, set to Ruth Brown's "Oh What A Dream," I wanted to express that, in many ways, the suffering and demoralizing of women is something that's shared. I set about to tell one story by seven women to express a commonality, a shared experience, by virtue of the fact of being a woman. I spent time in rehearsal speaking with the dancers about this because I wanted them to not only understand but also contribute to what they were dancing. Their ways of relating to the issue were unlike mine, mainly due to our age difference, but they all had stories about the pain and the marginalization they'd felt in certain scenarios.

To highlight the importance of the dancers' personal stories, I asked each of them to create a sixteen-count phrase that depicted some aspect of their experience. From these, we built a structure. Once the structure was in place, I designed the space so that there were times when one of them was "speaking" and other times when three or five of them were. Regardless of who was dancing, their stories meshed, gathered power together, and were presented as if coming from one voice.

This section ended up being quite beautiful visually. We lit only from side lights downstage so that, if a dancer moved upstage, she moved into the darkness. This enabled the dancers to jump into and out of the "conversation" by just appearing and disappearing. The screen over their heads depicted a single image of Mary, painted by James Christensen, entitled *Annunciation*. I used it here specifically because her hair and dress look contemporary, and she appears to be about the age of my student dancers. I love this section because it was a true collaboration between myself and my students.

As this dance breaks up, the UPS man comes back onto the stage as a sort of transition but also to continue his story. He walks among the dancers with his package as they leave the stage, inquiring as he passes people. Simultaneously, the wooden cross frame is lowered, and one dancer stands behind the portal looking toward the stage and audience. In this section, to the music "In the Still of the Night," two dancers begin moving in the upstage left corner in a duet created to express philos, which is a chaste love or could resemble friendship.

Remember that duet from the previous summer? The one that got me thinking about using music from the 1950s? With some minor edits and corrections, it slipped beautifully into place. It's like it was made to go here, I just didn't know that at the time. Creating out of order seems to happen so often in composition, and it never loses its miracle-like properties.

When I teach dance composition, I frequently refer to the quote that is often (perhaps incorrectly) attributed to Michelangelo, "I saw the angel in the marble, and I carved until I set him free." So many times, you can feel that the art is around you or in you. You just have to set it free. You just need human bodies through which to express it. These tiny miracles expose the omnipresence of art and how it lives among and between us just waiting to be accessed. At the end of this piece, the two exit by way of the frame and disappear into darkness as the solitary dancer who was watching comes through the frame to the stage.

After the dancer steps through the frame and enters the stage, the frame flies out, as if she's come through a portal that closes behind her. Simultaneously, the projection screen crosses into the space, filling the void left by the frame. For a while, I'd been mulling over ideas related to Sisyphus and his task for eternity to roll a boulder up a hill only to have it roll back down. This related to my research (and personal feelings) concerning the seemingly never-ending misogyny that comes along with being a woman. The slights, the micro-aggressions are so ingrained into everyday life that in some cases, we stop even seeing them. It's exhausting.

I was mulling over this idea and how it relates to dance because of its physicality and, while it seems counterintuitive, I thought this might be the place for a little levity. So this solo involves one dancer, repetition of specific phraseology, and a bag of balloons. We played with this idea

PROCESS, AN EXAMPLE   29

of a goal-oriented task—blowing up the balloon—and all the many different ways that others could derail it. I had other dancers enter the stage in various places. After she stretched, blew, and tied it, they pop the balloon, which leads to her having to start all over again. A single image projected onto the screen, also a nod to lightheartedness, was *Modern Annunciation* by Gottfried Helnwein. It depicts a very young woman sitting close to a 1950s TV screen, white light glaring out into a darkened room. From out of the TV, an angel is reaching toward the girl. As the piece ends, the music fades out as does the image, and the dancer is laying on her back on the floor with a blown-up balloon that she pinches closed and holds over her head with a straight arm. When she releases it, the balloon flies all over the stage as it releases air, like a giant, audible sign.

As part of the transition to the next piece, the platform made for *Acquiescence* is rolled onstage. I liked this set piece, but I wanted to incorporate it better and have it present not just for practical purposes (although it was important in that way) but also to serve as a cast member. I wanted it to be seamlessly integrated as a way to show time, place, and travel. I wanted it to appear and disappear just as the dancers do. I opted to change it from a square to a circle. It was still about six feet in diameter and a bit over a foot off the ground.

I felt a circle fit more with the piece because it was a metaphor for a clock, time passing, childbearing years, the cyclical nature of women's fertility, and the roundness of a pregnant or not pregnant belly. It was mounted to wheels and incorporated air castors so it could be clamped down or free to roll. It provided another layer of context and also a conveyance between and within the story. As this set piece was placed, the UPS man entered again, this time from a different wing and with growing frustration that he can't find the owner of the box. Until he happens upon her, he is lost and meandering with the box.

By the time he exits, the stage is set for Marie Howe's gorgeous poem. The woman laying on the floor gets up and walks to the platform, and this time (as opposed to the previous incarnation of this poem), the circular platform is turned and manipulated by dancers in the cast. She speaks the poem as the wheel is turned and she is moved into and out of the sidelight. This is the second person who uses vocalization in this work. Interestingly, the only two people who speak are the box carrier and the woman who will eventually receive the box. As the poem ends and the platform is silenced, she begins to trace the outline of the circle through her steps, and Johnny Mathis' "Chances Are" fades up.

This portion of the piece uses the "Ave Maria" section of *Acquiescence* as inspiration. Dancers walk around the outside of the platform until one by one they move onto the platform to create interpretations of the depictions of various Annunciation paintings that are being projected onto the screen. This section of the piece is slow-moving and contemplative, a stark contrast from everything presented previously. The images shown, created by a variety of artists, differ in style and tone. They were chosen to represent a wide cross section of different cultures' depictions of the biblical story. The projection of images continues as the music shifts to The Harptones' "A Sunday Kind of Love," and eventually the dancers move off the platform to individual solos that occur simultaneously. This piece ends in silence with eight dancers standing and facing into the platform. During this silent transition, the screen flies out and the dancers break into two groups, one group of three who manipulate the platform and the other five who create a lift that is reminiscent of the crucifixion. This lift is held while the platform is pushed upstage right in silence. Halfway there, we hear the first notes of the Isley Brothers, "Shout."

I created this *Shout* section to portray *agape* or divine love, so I created a glorious group work filled with buoyant movements, such as big jumps and low rolls. I set out to create a joyous romp that looks like it's celebrating God's love for people and people's love for God. Once created, it also reminded me almost of an experience of religious ecstasy or Pentecostal-type "slaying of the spirit" movements. To create this massive love fest, I challenged myself to use all of the dancers and to fill the entire stage with specific phraseology that looked riotous.

This section can most accurately be described as organized chaos. It is six minutes of high-powered, fast-tempo jumps, rolls, and canons. Dancers run from one phrase to the other in an almost manic way. It feels reminiscent of the Tarantella (but in a chaste format). I used the large dance section from the original *Acquiescence* as a base, which was very interesting considering that in the first iteration, the choreography had a bound, heavy impression, giving the audience the sense that the dancers' movements were arduous and restricted. Because I had so many

PROCESS, AN EXAMPLE 31

dancers, I was able to play with groups splitting and reforming, bringing dancers who are performing disparate phrases to suddenly join together to form a new group. The timing was altered, facings and directions switched up, and so much was evolving, growing, and shrinking that it felt hard to keep up with the dance visually.

I pulled movement motifs and excerpted segments from the first and second section of this piece (*Johnny B Goode* and *Oh What a Dream*) and interlaced them with base phrases. The turntable on wheels performed its role first in the downstage left corner, as dancers moved onto it and held positions from the previous *Chances Are* section, and then the dancer moved off to join the larger dance only to be replaced by another. During what may be the only quiet moment, the platform was pushed slowly across the stage by half the cast while the other half moved on it from one held position to another only to burst into frenzied movement when it touched the other side of the stage. It was later moved upstage (and into what is usually the theater shop), and dancers took turns moving on and off of it while the heart of the dance raged downstage. The piece slowly devolves into visual chaos as the music gets wilder. As the music begins to fade out, the UPS man returns and is buffeted around by the chaotic movement, and all eventually end up off stage except for one dancer who is lying on the floor. Slowly the frame descends as the music rises for the next section.

The next section represents *eros* or romantic love. Since the dancer who is lying down is the same person who danced with the balloons and will, eventually, accept the box, I decided to leave her on stage as an observer instead of giving her the duet to dance. It bears mentioning here that I didn't set out to tell the story of the Annunciation *per se*. Therefore, the choices that I made didn't necessarily reflect the bible narrative or textual analysis or really anything other than my thoughts on the subject. For example, there is much debate about the alleged virginity of Mary and whether that matters or not in regard to the birth of Jesus. This debate, while central to the account of the Annunciation, isn't pertinent to my interpretation of this story.

I chose here to depict a romantic relationship and place the dancer depicting Mary off to the side so that she sees the relationship unfold. I leave it up to the observer to decide for themselves if a romantic relationship matters to her, if the woman dancer is actually her and she's watching herself, if she sacrificed in this regard, or if the question of a relationship is even of consequence. As she moves to the side, one dancer enters the stage through the frame and another from the wings. The observer sits downstage with her back to the audience as if she is one of them. They move together to Etta James' "At Last" as the lights dim and focus on them. As the piece concludes, the couple crosses the stage walking hand in hand as the observer counter-crosses in front of them, watching, to reach stage left. This is the first counter-crossing of the stage that we see this character make. The very obvious going-against-the-tide image is clearly meant to signify that she sees what others are doing and moves on her own path.

The final section of this piece contains many elements. It begins as a solo set to "Mona Lisa" by Nate King Cole. The screen lowers, and an image of the *Annunciation* by Henry Ossawa Tanner is shown. As the music segues to an instrumental interlude, the screen rises, the platform is rolled downstage center, and the UPS man enters from upstage left. As she dances, he looks for her. She sees him as he walks downstage to stand on the platform. She stops dancing and moves to stand on the opposite side of the platform, and it begins to slowly spin. Through gesture and facial expression, but in silence, he relates that he's looking for someone, and he asks her if the box is hers. In a very tiny, yet for me, probably the most poignant moment in the dance—she pauses and considers.

This is the moment that makes this story a feminist one. This was the moment that I had poured two years of my life into making. She's asked a question, and she thinks about it. At that moment, the answer is her own. It's almost irrelevant whether she chooses to accept or not. It's the fact that she has a choice that is important. Her agency and power are reflected in this tiny moment. There have been many articles written about this story from many religious and disciplinary perspectives, including one that looks at the mother of God in light of the #MeToo movement. I delved into these writings and deeply considered the arguments. Ultimately though, I decided for myself what was important to me and what spoke to me. My response never pretended to be anything other than a very personal reading.

To be specific about the part of the Mary story I'm discussing, below is an excerpt from the Book of Luke, Chapter 1:

> 26 In the sixth month, the angel Gabriel was sent from God to a town of Galilee called Nazareth,

PROCESS, AN EXAMPLE   33

27 to a virgin betrothed to a man named Joseph, of the house of David, and the virgin's name was Mary.

28 And coming to her, he said, "Hail, favored one! The Lord is with you."

29 But she was greatly troubled at what was said and pondered what sort of greeting this might be.

30 Then the angel said to her, "Do not be afraid, Mary, for you have found favor with God.

31 Behold, you will conceive in your womb and bear a son, and you shall name him Jesus.

32 He will be great and will be called Son of the Most High, and the Lord God will give him the throne of David his father,

33 and he will rule over the house of Jacob forever, and of his kingdom there will be no end."

34 But Mary said to the angel, "How can this be, since I have no relations with a man?"

35 And the angel said to her in reply, "The holy Spirit will come upon you, and the power of the Most High will over-shadow you. Therefore the child to be born will be called holy, the Son of God.

36 And behold, Elizabeth, your relative, has also conceived a son in her old age, and this is the sixth month for her who was called barren;

37 for nothing will be impossible for God."

38 Mary said, "Behold, I am the handmaid of the Lord. May it be done to me according to your word." Then the angel departed from her.[3]

Between lines 37 and 38 lie the heart of this entire dance work. The space between those two lines contains a wealth of meaning, a universe of contemplation. She paused and considered. She could have decided to say no. She is powerful. This future is one that she chooses for herself. And so in the dance, she takes the box he offers (the first sign of acceptance), opens it (a second sign of acceptance), and a helium balloon rises slowly from it on a long string. She watches as it rises into the sky as if she's seeing her future play out. She takes the balloon (a third sign of acceptance) and steps off the platform, and it rolls away with the UPS man aboard.

PROCESS, AN EXAMPLE

The piece then becomes a duet between her and the balloon, her and her chosen future, perhaps. She leans one way, and, by virtue of its helium core, it moves the other direction. She holds tight to the balloon and turns, and the string flies out and then wraps around her. She walks her hands up the string, and the balloon descends toward her. This duet is concerned with introductions, learning about each other, and communicating in the way that an expectant mother might cradle her belly or feel the kick of her baby. As the piece continues, we see a line of dancers walking single file, slowly upstage left to upstage right, toward a single offstage light.

As the music begins to fade, the solo dancer takes the balloon string and ties it around her waist. This image is important as it reflects Renaissance painters' use of a bow tied at the waist to signify a woman is with a child. In the silence, she walks slowly stage left, string tied at her waist, balloon suspended above her head. I like this imagery of moving against the current. It reinforces the feminist lens that I've used with this piece. Her choice put her at odds with the majority of people, and her power allows her to move forward. The two groups walk their separate ways as the lights fade.

I'm always very aware that my students are not just watching my creative process but many times contributing and certainly learning and performing it. Because every part of the process fosters kinesthetic, emotional, and intellectual growth, I discuss not just movement shapes, effort, time, and all the other elements that comprise composition and performance but also the thematic material; its origins, its relationship to movement phrases, and why I change or choose to leave phrases, sections, groupings as I do. I spend time discussing the title as well; whether it should add further mystery to the poetic shapes on display, if it should illuminate or educate, or if it's necessary at all.

I called this work *The 25th of March*, which is the date that the Annunciation is celebrated in the Christian Church. This particular title referred more literally to the subject of the piece than the titles of some of my other works. I felt the movement phraseology and the story that I was telling were a bit opaque, and I wanted to give the audience something to grasp.

VIDEO REFERENCE 1.3

The 25th of March

Again, as I stated earlier, showing work to an audience in a fully produced format gives the choreographer the chance to see the piece through new eyes. As usual, sitting in the audience and watching this work gave me perspective, gave me the forest instead of the trees, and I made notes with the plan of resetting this again. Dramaturgical questions arose such as the choice to have one performer speaking and serving more as an actor than a dancer, the role of comedy in this work, and issues of abstraction or lack thereof. I reflected on performance-related issues, such as costume design, projection choice, and the moving platform, which had the potential to be dangerous.

The main issue I had with the *25th of March* was that the production elements were very separate from the dance. A screen came down, and an image was projected, and that image was defined by the limits of the screen and, in most cases, high above the heads of the dancers. I sought to integrate the two elements of dance and image, at least in portions of the piece. I was also very interested in projecting video as well as still images and felt it would be an interesting artistic challenge.

A secondary issue was the role of the UPS man. The actor who portrayed this role was wonderful, but the live speech on stage didn't flow with the dance in the way that I envisioned. Instead of speech and movement supporting each other's mode of performance, they seemed disparate. I resolved to use a dancer in the next iteration and see if the story flowed better. Similarly, I wasn't thrilled with the poem being spoken. I think if speaking occurred throughout this piece, it wouldn't have bothered me. But as it was (apart from the student dancer's beautiful performance of the poem), the act of having the poem read during the piece seemed out of place dramatically.

I invited a few respected colleagues to see the work and give feedback and was gratified to be able to speak with choreographers and dance and religion faculty about it and receive important critical response from people not intimately associated with the piece. I took this feedback and decided to give myself one year as the deadline for a final version of this piece.

M(other)

Figure 1.5 M(other).
Credit: ©Washington and Lee University, 2016.

In revising this choreographic work, I decided to begin with an entirely new piece of music. The goal of the first section was the same as the first section of *The 25th of March*, to introduce the characters, the UPS man, the dancers, a specific dancer who appears with the group but is different, and to demonstrate that the UPS man was looking for the person intended to receive his box, but he wasn't sure who it was. Set to "Come Go With Me" by The Del Vikings, the curtain rose to reveal a spotlight on the ground that immediately began to search the stage, sweeping down and across to land on a brown box. The UPS man steps out of the darkness and begins a duet with the box where it's evident he's searching on the box to find an address, a name, some indication of where it goes.

While his duet continues, in a similar way to the first iteration of this piece, dancers enter in a very relaxed manner. They are walking and interacting almost as they would do behind the curtain prior to a performance. They are chatting, slowly moving, and in some cases stretching or standing. The UPS man begins to interact with them, seeking the owner of his box. Because the cast is fairly large with thirteen dancers, this serves to introduce the stage space to the audience. As indicated in the first iteration of this piece, we used the full stage including the theater shop behind the stage, concrete walls, and all the legs and masking for the boom and overhead lights are flown out so the entire space is revealed.

As the piece progresses, some dancers bring out large flats that are about three feet by ten feet. They appear to be carrying them from one side of the stage to the other, but they stop and pause and sit them down. Video is projected onto them of static that you might see on an old TV set, along with the number countdown that used to be the prelude to the start of old black-and-white movies. All of these symbols allude to the fact that this section is an overture, an introduction, and the cast of characters. The very end of this section has a nice little piece of foreshadowing when three flats are brought onto the stage within a few seconds of one another. A balloon image is projected onto the middle of the first flat, then the second flat is brought on and "catches" the balloon toward the top of the flat, and the third flat is brought on and is raised high into the air to "catch" the balloon before it flies offstage.

The transition between sections here changed a bit from the last version. I made Oh What A Dream more fluid as the large group transitions off stage and leaves two to dance the next sequence. To further aid in creating a seamless story, a frame does not descend from the fly space, but rather the images for the second section of this dance are projected onto the back wall of the theater. Because what serves as the back wall is a large metal garage door and concrete blocks, the images take on the accordion shape of the metal door and the texture of the cinderblocks that make up the area around the door. This is interesting because it gives a rough edge to the masterful artworks that are being projected. I loved the contrast.

Although our projectors had the capability to fill the entire back wall, I chose for this piece to project just above the heads of the dancers. While this may seem a departure given that my goal was for the dancers to perform inside the images, the nature of this section of the piece required the dancers to be in complete darkness while standing on stage and waiting for their various entrances into the light. Had I not raised the projection up a bit, a major component of the visual impact of the piece would have been shattered because the dancers meant to be in darkness would have been bathed in the light of the large-scale projected images.

The next section, In the Still of the Night, which was originally a 1950s-inspired duet involving a man and a woman, was changed to reflect a duet by two women. I felt that upending the gender balance would give this piece added depth, and I love that philos is expressed here by two people of the same gender, but danced as a stereotypical duet. It also reflects the fact that a woman need not be contrasted with a man to show power. Both of these characters' phrases exhibit power in varied ways. I modified bits of choreography here and there for fluidity and to fit these specific dancers' strengths.

I switched up the order of the sections here. Originally, the section blowing up the balloons happened here. I moved it to later in the dance because I felt like the mood created by the Oh What A Dream section was very beautiful, soft, and gentle, and it was a bit jarring to lunge into a silly interlude. What I put next is the poem on the circular platform on wheels. Our amazing production team created a new, better, and safer platform for us. They purchased new pneumatic wheels, which were smaller and had a lower profile so the entire platform could be lower to the ground. They custom-built handles all around the edges of the platform for easy moving without having to grab onto the flat where the dancers walked, and they removed the black curtain material from the outside and custom-fit black wooden pieces around the edges so that the set was sleeker. The platform was brought on stage in the dark as the prior piece was ending, and instead of the dancer speaking, the poem was recorded. Also, in what I feel is one of the most beautiful moments in the piece, excerpts, words, and word pictures were projected onto the back wall of the stage while the recorded poem was played. Simultaneously, the platform was being turned, bringing the dancer into and out of the light.

A fluid segue out of the poem in the last version of this piece was a large movement sequence set to "Chances Are" and "Sunday Kind of Love." I changed the music in the first section to "Only You" by the Platters. I never really liked "Chances Are" as a song so used this opportunity to find something that I felt fit better with the movement, and I cut the entire Sunday Kind of Love section. The two pieces together went on too long. Watching it later with a critical eye that was a few months removed, I felt

PROCESS, AN EXAMPLE   39

that I was hitting the audience over the head with the thematic material that flowed from the art/poses connection, such as the five dancers who create a lift reminiscent of the angel hovering above the ground speaking to Mary. The section said the same thing over and over. I always tell my students to beware of dictating to the audience and of repeating themselves. Audiences are smart. They will absorb and translate it for themselves. Wasn't it Doris Humphrey who said, "All dances are too long"? Yeah. I never missed the second section that I cut.

I think one of the most beautiful elements of this section of the piece was the projections. We got a very long and wide lens and set up a projector hanging from a truss over the audience, so we were able to project the paintings of the Annunciation onto the entire back wall of the stage. Additionally, while the dance was ongoing on the circular platform, other dancers brought in the large white flats from the first section. Anytime that a dancer stopped and held their flat facing the audience, that portion of the painting would be picked up and would stand out in relief from the back wall. I used this very beautiful methodology to highlight areas of the paintings that I wanted to receive extra attention. When the flat was turned ninety degrees to face offstage, it practically disappeared. As the images changed, the dancers moved to various places upstage and down and moved within the artwork. This was a beautiful culmination of my desire to dance "inside" the artworks. It was challenging technically because all of the positions had to be spiked and the dancers had to remember how high they were holding the flats, where on the flat to grasp, and at what angle, and all of this had to be timed to the music. It was a wonderful challenge.

The final forty-five seconds of this section took place in silence and then segued to "Stay" by the Zodiacs and Maurice Williams. I hadn't intended to make any new sections of choreography, but the idea of projecting video and using the flats to pick up parts that I wanted to highlight was just too tempting to pass up. At the end of the previous section, all the dancers on the platform each took a flat and positioned them out toward the audience (hiding their bodies), touching side to side with one another so that the round platform became a five-sided mirror ball of sorts. As the platform was pushed downstage and turned while it was in motion, video from other sections of the dance were projected onto the flats the dancers were holding. Other videos of the dance were simultaneously projected on the back wall and on other individual flats positioned and moving around the stage.

We also used a video from *The 25th of March* as part of the projections as an homage to the original cast. The flats in this section served as additional cast members. They were great monoliths that moved with grace and were raised or lowered depending on where they were on stage and within the music. It seemed effortless when watching but, in reality, it was both quite complicated to organize and heavy for the dancers to carry. All of this happened while other dancers moved in front of and behind the flats, thus in front of and behind the videos, with new phraseology intermixed with some combinations we've seen before and others that occur later in the piece.

One lovely moment of foreshadowing was the video from the previous year of the scene that took place on the platform when the UPS man finally finds the girl and gives the box. This was nice because the audience doesn't know that they will see this yet, and it was a lovely reminder of the two dancers who had created those roles and had since graduated. This was a

Figure 1.6 M(other).
Credit: ©Washington and Lee University, 2016.

Figure 1.7 M(other).
Credit: ©Washington and Lee University, 2016.

scary piece to put together because we never really knew what it looked like until tech week. I have to give tons of credit to my colleague and lighting designer, Shawn Paul Evans. His work is an example of what can be achieved when designers and choreographers work well together and honor and respect one another. Plus, he is the most patient human on the planet and a supremely gifted artist, which is wonderful. This piece fades away as the platform is moved to the center and the dancers mount it for *Shout*.

I left *Shout* relatively the same. I had a different cast, so I altered some formations and placements. Because of the improved platform, the lifts and dancing that occurred on it while it was moving were smoother and looked less precarious. I was able to fix small problematic areas. After reviewing the piece again for this book, I do wish I had incorporated gender-neutral clothing or at least put one of the men dancers in a white dress and a few of the women dancers in pants. It's quite gendered as it is. I think this is a holdover from the first iteration that strove to overlay 1950s imagery onto a feminist story. In creating that juxtaposition, I inadvertently might have undermined my theme. It bears thinking about, definitely.

PROCESS, AN EXAMPLE

One difference in this section is that I didn't use the far upstage scene shop for part of the dance. Originally, the scene shop doors were open during this section because we rear projected onto the screen. In the second iteration, the projections were front projected, so we could close the shop door. This meant that the platform couldn't be stored in the open shop door between sections so it had to be built to fit between the side lights so it could go offstage when not in use. It made for a cleaner if not deeper stage. Next, I slotted in the balloon section. *Shout* is such a happy free-for-all that this silly section was well placed and didn't cause a sharp contrast in feel as it had done the previous year. The smiling faces of the audience carried over to *If I Give My Heart to You*. It remained the same although the new dancer added some of her own small touches.

Watching it all again as I prepare this book, I'm not loving that the next piece is *At Last*. There is a sharp contrast in tone here because of the previous balloon section. I don't know. Maybe that's OK. Scenically, we did a nice job of lighting and using Gobo transitions to change the timbre. The transition, though, is a bit harsh, dance-wise. If I ever set this again, I will look to make a change of some sort here.

This section is the *eros* exploration, and the choreography remains basically the same except for some modifications to fix funky choreographic elements and attune the piece to the new dancers. This version of this dance piece follows the same story as the original version but in a looser way. The dance was choreographed to sometimes allow the dancers to break out of assigned roles. For example, the UPS man dances in *Shout* (albeit with a costume change). In this version, instead of sitting and watching this love duet from the audiences' point of view, the Mary character performs it with a male partner. I made this choice to highlight that she was a normal woman in every way. It presented the question of her wanting and/or having romantic relationships.

Having the dancer who plays the role of Mary perform the duet worked better for the next transition. At the end of the section, the two dancers in the duet began to walk off the stage, hand-in-hand, and at about center stage, she lets go of his hand and stops, and he continues off. It made for a nice transition into the next section. Also, it could be interpreted as another moment of choice where she decides that *eros* isn't what she wants. Or conversely, maybe the solo that follows represents an

PROCESS, AN EXAMPLE   43

inner monologue, a joy at the prospect of a love relationship. I like that there could be many interpretations of this. I also love that this version highlights the various choices that the Mary character has to make along the way and therefore makes the eventual ending more poignant.

This new transition leads to *Mona Lisa*, which I left pretty much the same. One difference is that the image is now projected across the entire back of the stage and is riddled with the imprint of the flaws in the wall. Because we are front projecting, it reaches all the way to the stage floor and up into the fly space. I love this large image and that she is, in effect, dancing within it. Because the shop door is closed and the rolling platform is, at this moment, stored offstage, the entrance of the UPS man and platform is slightly different. He is standing frozen on the platform as it is rolled onstage from the wings by the dancers. I love that our set designer put handles all along the sides of the platform because it allows the stagehands to remain in one place while turning the platform during the "conversation" between the UPS man and Mary.

This section continues with the duet between the dancer and the balloon. It's very close, choreographically, to the last version with small tweaks for this particular dancer. I made a small music edit at the end of the piece to extend the music a little. I didn't like that the previous version ended in silence. That gave the piece a bit of a melancholy feel. This small extension of music meant that the music continued as the dancers crisscrossed walking off and ended as the lights came down. A better period at the end of the sentence.

This very long and detailed depiction of my dance doesn't really include much about the costumes, save the UPS man. In all the iterations of this dance, the costumes were fairly simple. Of course, they grew and developed with each version of the dance, but they all had basics in common. *Acquiescence* featured pale blue, baby-doll style dresses. This choice was a reference to the color of the garments worn by Mary in the images of stained-glass windows. The style was a nod to youthfulness. The costumes gave the impression of innocence and fragility, which contrasted sharply with the movement style.

For the original *B-Side* dance, the costumes were typical 1950s Americana. The dress was a bright yellow fit and flare with a full skirt that fell just below the knee. Her partner wore a khaki pant with a

PROCESS, AN EXAMPLE

fitted button-down collared shirt. Later iterations of the dance alluded to this style but were a bit more abstract. We stayed with the fit and flare look, but each dancer's dress was slightly different from the rest in the neckline, sleeve length, or fabric embellishments, which gave them individuality. We decided to construct all the dresses out of variations of white to reflect innocence. The fabric was light, so as the dancers moved, the air caught it and flowed through it. There were many layers of fabric in the skirts, so there was a lush quality about them. The costumes could be interpreted as wedding or first communion dresses but as the style was to the knee with a belted waist, they were an abstracted idea of these connotations. I liked the ceremonial feel of this and still enjoy the delicate look juxtaposed against the powerful movement. In the final version of the dance, we added many layers of fabric under the skirts, both as a nod to the 1950s style and so that the skirts had more movement as they flowed through space.

I chose to change the title of this piece to m(other). Resetting and editing this piece helped me to understand more clearly what I felt and what I wanted to say. As I moved through the choreography a year after the first performance and a few years from the original idea, it became increasingly apparent that this wasn't about a specific biblical story, although the dance was told through that lens. I reinterpreted a story that some perceive as a patriarchal narrative that celebrates submissiveness, gentleness, and quietness. Present in that patriarchal viewpoint are all sorts of outdated views on women including deference to the male hierarchy.

The androcentric retelling of what is at its heart a woman's story and the Renaissance art that, for the most part, reinforced the male perspective provided a base against which to react. The fight was against being treated as "other." It was against the idea that woman is "less than" and one who doesn't deserve a voice, an opinion, or a choice. "Other" has the choice made for them by those who view themselves as powerful or righteous. The fight (my fight) wasn't necessary to point out the masculine point of view and the inherently unfair depiction of the story. I was interested in the woman and what I view as a single empowering moment.

It interested me that this moment is not acknowledged (or maybe even noticed) in many philosophical and religious writings on the topic.

It struck me that maybe the lack of attention is purposeful because, in this one small moment, a woman has agency. While I play with the Archangel Gabriel's identity by making him a UPS man who doesn't know whom he is looking for, the significance of the piece is that she does know. In my version, she sees and understands. She questions and contemplates. She weighs options and decides.

In so many ways, my earlier research on the intersection of motherhood and modern dance played a large role in this final production. Choosing motherhood can be a difficult decision for any woman. As a dancer, your livelihood depends upon you getting into and out of the physical "effects" of motherhood as soon as possible. Afterward, your livelihood challenges your role as a mother in terms of time, financial strain, energy, body consciousness, and a host of other stresses. Teaching or dancing professionally while also being a mother is unusual because the reasons above contribute to you standing apart from your peers, requiring different allowances, and needing different types of support. Quickly, it is easy to become "other" when you work and live in a dancer's body. This contradiction was also present in my biblical story. The Mary character willingly chooses to set herself apart. She becomes not just *other* but by virtue of her child, m(*other*).

VIDEO REFERENCE 1.4

M(other)

Notes

1 "The Annunciation" Copyright © 2009 by Marie Howe.
2 "The Annunciation" Copyright © 2009 by Marie Howe.
3 Luke 1: 26–38 (New American Bible).

2

WHAT IS *NOT* DANCE?

Figure 2.1 Breathing Lessons.
Credit: ©Washington and Lee University, 2013.

DOI: 10.4324/9780367824167-3

WHAT IS *NOT* DANCE?   47

While not simple, it is within the scope of most people's experience to discuss what dance is. Defining it usually consists of a common vocabulary. Movement in time. Neuromuscular impulses. Body moving through space. In most cases, an agreement among a classroom is fairly routine. What can be difficult to discuss is what dance isn't. I typically ask this question during the first week of the semester to get our creative minds moving and also to encourage students to delve deeply into their personal beliefs, suppositions and, potentially, their prejudices. Many times, they don't even realize they have strong opinions on the subject until I begin asking very specific questions.

This discussion at this particular time is very helpful as it coincides with me getting to know my students and learning what sort of dance background they have (if any). Based on their responses, it doesn't take long at all to determine who has had a classical education, those that practiced non-traditional dance methods, those who have no experience but love watching dance, and students who have experience in other art forms. There are always a few students who fit in none of these categories and, more often than not, they tend to contribute fascinating thoughts and opinions. Not being influenced by prior dance classes or performance experiences allows these students to be free in their thinking and imagination and enables them to connect disparate concepts without the burden of experience.

While it may sound odd to describe experience as a burden, new college students have only their training up to that point to shape their view of dance and, usually, haven't been exposed to much. They sometimes subconsciously begin their collegiate education thinking that their specific experience in dance is all that there is. It takes a bit of time (and sometimes it's quite difficult) to broaden their horizons and show them that their narrow experience is just that.

Some of the most interesting discussions that I've had in class are a result of inquiring "To be a dance, must the body move?" or "Can stillness be a dance?" Of course, to dance educators, the work of Judson Dance Theatre and others asked these very questions and answered them through their experimentation and performance, but generally, this question sparks lively conversation among students. Similarly, "If I sit on the edge of the stage and eat a sandwich, did I just dance?" elicits giggles at first but tends to cause a mental double take when I add, "What if I created lighting cues for my sandwich eating and had a costume designed for it?" and later "What if I planned the specific nature of my bites to go left to right from the bottom of my sandwich up, and when I reached halfway, flipped the sandwich over and finished it in two big bites? Did I choreograph the eating? Is this a dance?"

Once they seem to reach an agreement or a comfortable disagreement, I ask, "What if I did exactly the same eating pattern in my costume sitting in the park? Is this a dance?" and "What if I have no eating pattern or costume but next to me in the park I put a sign that said This is a dance?" And later "How is the park different from sitting on the edge of the stage? Must you have a theater to have a dance? Must you have movement? What role does the audience play in dance? Must they be present?" Similarly, the questions "Must there be a human involved for something to be considered a dance?" and "Do bees dance? Can robots?" seem to be very simple until they are considered more closely.

Once the group has talked it out, I use online resources to show them videos of Judson Dance Theatre members dancing through these exact questions. Later, when the class structure and the students are comfortable, we delve deeper by looking at societal and cultural norms and discuss their place in the larger consideration of what dance is. We highlight personal bias and try to shed light on why our opinions have formed as they have, how they can be expanded and more inclusive, and what our obligations and responsibilities are as choreographers.

The dialectic nature of my class hinges on students having varying opinions, and I've never been disappointed. Of course, every class is different but, generally, these questions help the students to develop a natural investigatory process that is specific to themselves as distinct individuals in this specific class. I work so that the process is one they are both comfortable with and that also serves the needs of the course. This is the framework upon which the class is hung. I use this structure repeatedly throughout the semester.

3

VOCABULARY

Figure 3.1 Aerial Bungee Performance.
Credit: ©Washington and Lee University, 2013.

Students enroll in a composition class for a variety of different reasons. Some have a lot of dance experience but have never created work, others sign up because it sounds interesting but have no experience with composition or dance, and others are merely working toward fulfilling their required arts credits. It can be daunting to have such a wide experience and interest level in one class. In addition, these elements contain the added complexity of each individual's personal biases, their culture background, and their educational history. Their experiences before they walk into the dance studio are imprinted on them and, if not brought to light, can unintentionally guide their thought processes and decision-making.

Because students bring to my classroom a variety of backgrounds and experiences, I find it useful to spend time creating a common vocabulary. Words and concepts relating to art tend to be used and shared without a deep understanding of their meaning. Everyone thinks they know, for example, what creativity is but few people can describe it. The more abstract and conceptual the terms are, the more elusive their stated definitions may prove be. Terms also can have meanings that differ based on an individuals' experiences, or their cultural or societal norms. This ambiguity can be confusing and potentially derail conversation. Before meaningful work can be created, it's important to bridge this chasm of vaguery and misconception to shape communication and generate a shared understanding of words.

At the very beginning of the semester, I start with a conversation about the defining of words. Everyone shares in the creation of the definitions, and a vocabulary list of terms is developed. At the start, I don't focus on traditionally accepted or defined answers in this exercise. Instead, group sharing and discussion lead to honing and ultimate agreement on the answers. This is accomplished by me remaining a moderator only, shaping the discussion, pointing out potential flaws in logic, and moving the conversation toward consensus. This encourages the students' agency, so they actively contribute to the process, and it emboldens them to share broadly while also listening to others' perspectives. Often, knee-jerk reactions are tempered by other points of view, discussion and debate occurs, and a more nuanced reply grows. The group works together to solve a problem by using critical thinking skills and simultaneously creating the base from which the rest of the semester will spring. This democratic practice creates equity in the classroom by giving all the students, regardless of dance experience, an equal contribution to the language we will use throughout the semester. It also highlights the capacity of dance and dance language to be molded and shaped as its elastic nature includes all of those in the room.

The particular words that I choose to emphasize are generally overarching and broad. They challenge the students to create a few sentences to describe topics about which authors have written entire books. This process seeks to dispel myths and helps the group to see their limitations, biases, and personal views of artmaking prior to the start of composing.

I usually begin by asking them to define "art." Of course, this is a huge task and based on how the students deal with this question, I can begin to learn more about them as people and artist/students. Usually, a few speak up immediately and say something like, "Art is the creation of something beautiful." (I initially skip over the very loaded "beauty" word and move on, knowing we will come back to it and not wanting to stop the flow of ideas.) I write down everyone's ideas on a whiteboard. Generally, there are portions of overlap in answers, and I point those out. In this way, I am finding commonalties, but I keep asking questions based on their responses in order to move the group out of the simplistic realm of "pictures that hang on museum walls" and into the intangible arena of "the shaping of materials." Eventually someone throws out the word "aesthetic." This is an exciting moment because not only is it part of the definition of art but also it leads us to the next word that we need to define as a group. We continue in this manner, defining words that we will need to understand in order to define other words. As we move along, the terms become increasingly more dance specific and later more choreographically specific. The students will see and use these terms again as we apply our flowchart to the choreographic process and begin to make work. (More information on the flowchart will appear in Chapter 5.) Typically, I orchestrate the process of inquiry to flow from:

Art → Aesthetics → Beauty → Creativity → Communication →
Intent → Composition → Movement → Body

52   VOCABULARY

After discussion and refining, the students' group responses tend to look something like this:

- Art: the shaping of material, creating an extraordinary experience, expression, creative skill, communicating an idea or story or feeling, an aesthetic experience, taking the ordinary and altering it, human skill, making something powerful
- Aesthetics: having to do with feeling, experiencing something, understanding through emotions, sensing, non-intellectual, beauty
- Beauty: a quality that bring happiness, meaningful design, intense feelings, pleasing to the eye, appreciation, elegance
- Creativity: innovation, originality, taking ordinary things and changing them, creating something new
- Communication: a way to express the intent, transmit a story, idea or emotion, conveying something
- Intent: purpose, reason for design, foundation for the composition
- Composition: ordering movement in space and time, a process of assembling, structure and form, design for the purpose of expression/communication through movement
- Movement: a neuromuscular event, signals the brain sends to stimulate nerves that move the muscles, motion of the body, body moving in space and time
- Body: the instrument of expression

Engaging in this process with students exposes their biases and, once discovered, can help the group to understand the lens through which each of them discusses, creates, and responds to work. It also ensures that dancers skilled in dissimilar forms understand one another's terminology, that dancers and those with little or no experience are on the same page, and that they all grasp the tenor of the course. Additionally, encouraging the students to find answers and supporting the participative process is much a more effective educational tool than simply giving them my definitions of artistic concepts.

Collaboratively creating the vocabulary they will use throughout the class grants the students ownership and, because of this, they tend to invest themselves in the class deeply. This is not to say that all of the responses from every student become part of the final definition. Should one student, for example, relate that a required element of dance is music, I use this response to ask the larger question about music's relationship to dance. While it's possible that no student has ever considered if a movement piece must include music to be considered dance, the fact that I introduce this question gives them pause. After discussion and some guiding, the group forms conclusions that are appropriate for what we are setting out to achieve. So, through this investigative process, while a particular student's answer may have been initially erroneous or incomplete, the discussion of such, guided by my questions, eventually leads to an improved definition.

Following the initial grouping of definitions, we then move on to what it means to be a choreographer. We discuss the choreographer's job, and usually end up with something like "designing the body or bodies creatively in space and time with specific energy." We talk about how the choreographer finds inspiration, a question that could have a myriad of answers. We discuss improvisation, books, interviews, journaling, etc., and how the choreographer generates material from those sources. The concept of intent is paramount, and a discussion ensues that prepares the students for the future when they will cross the bridge from an intellectual exercise to an embodied one.

We spend time reflecting upon the differences between dance-as-art and dance-as-entertainment. Students usually have a lot to say about this. Many students will, interestingly, appear to play a role that protects the style of dance performed in a live music concert or at the Super Bowl, for example, not wanting it to have a less than artistic description but not knowing why they feel that way or why it should or shouldn't be labeled entertainment. I tell the story of being fresh out of graduate school at my first job, serving as artistic director for a small dance company. One day I received a call from the local newspaper asking me to comment on a story having to do with a strip club that the city was trying to shut down for "indecency." The women who worked there were fighting back, claiming that their dancing was art, and they were artists. The reporter wanted to know if I thought this strip club produced art. Walking a fine line, I responded that the main difference between art and entertainment is intent and that the dancers themselves would have to answer the question.

This story prompts lively discussion as the students usually have strong opinions about a strip club producing art. (Yet, most, if not all of the students have never been inside one. A further example of bias.) Animated conversations grow to include the similarities and differences of dancing at the opening ceremony at the Olympics, for example, to if cheerleading and Tik Tok dances fit in the world of concert dance. These discussions help reveal the students' biases, provide new information on the dance-as-entertainment/dance-as-art debate, and serves to deepen the definition of intent.

Having a deep conversation about how to use intent to shape movement is valuable, especially early on. Sometimes it's that leap that derails new choreographers. How do you get from "I want to express my sorrow at the loss of my grandmother" to movement? Spending time here with Effort/Shape (Laban theory) and watching and discussing a few examples (Martha Graham's *Lamentations* is perfect for this particular subject matter) helps them to see theory put into practice. This leads beautifully into a discourse on how to shape the material that's been generated. How do you express sadness through our bodies? I may ask, "Using effort/shape, show three positions that express sadness." And later, "Connect them into a three-part phrase." Once performed, the choreographers have something tangible that they can discuss and assess.

Using Liz Lerman's Critical Response Process,[1] we discuss choices and how those choices affected them as audience. This leads effortlessly into what I call "the dancers' toolbox," which is a compilation of design tools to inspire and help them get started: theme and variation, symmetry/asymmetry, accumulation, canon, etc. (See Chapter 5, E. Refinement, *Your Toolbox* for a fuller description.) I hand out a list of tools, which, I explain, is a living document, and ask them to layer specific tools onto their three-movement phrase. Again, because we are watching something tangible, we can comment and respond. We can try various options to see how they generate different audience responses.

After this exercise is complete, I sometimes assign as homework Daniel Nagrin's "'Rules' for Choreography" from his book *Choreography and the Specific Image* and ask them to respond to each rule. By reading their reactions to Nagrin's rules, I tend to know how much a student has absorbed, the extent to which their views have expanded, and how strong their personal opinions are. Like Nagrin, I also hope "that one by one what is said here will be revised, contradicted, and/or proved wrong."[2] I encourage honest debate. By asking my students to comment on the rules, I can see the students' critical thinking skills in action.

Harnessing social media

A common vocabulary is also valuable for audiences. I have been experimenting on and off over the past ten years with incorporating social media into dance performances as a way to engage audiences in learning how to speak about dance. My exploration began as a fun way to give the dancers another opportunity to practice using dance vocabulary and, specifically, to talk about what they were performing in the concert. It made sense to me that educating audiences in the same way could only broaden and deepen their dance experience and give them insight into what they were seeing at our performances. But I wanted to do it in an accessible way.

Figure 3.2 #Wludance.
Credit: ©Washington and Lee University, 2011.

The first year, we used intermission to tweet out facts about the dances and photos from backstage, and we encouraged people to tweet back with questions or comments. We included a QR code in the program and specific directions for less tech' savvy folks about how to download and install an app that would read the code. It was marginally successful the first year. There was some interaction from the students, but the faculty, parents, and community didn't participate to any great degree.

Feeling that this was possibly a generational issue, the next year, in order to improve participation, we tweeted from a laptop backstage and projected the tweets on the upstage cyclorama. In this way, even the people who didn't know how to use Twitter could read and follow along with the conversation. This led to some funny tweets from parents who, uninterested in participating in the educational aspect of the feed, sent shout-outs to their children who were performing. Inevitably, students started shouting out as well, and the dancers began responding from the green room.

The next year, I added Instagram to the feed and projected both it and Twitter feeds. In an effort to wrestle my educational goals back under control, I assigned someone to send out content-specific tweets that expressed thematic material about a dance or included context for pieces they saw. We also included mini-interviews with the chorographers which fulfilled an academic goal. Including Instagram meant that we could project larger photos and then include information pertaining to costumes or other visual elements in the performance.

Over the next few years, I used the #wludanceconcert hash tag and continued the project. Gradually, it seemed, people caught up with technology, and a larger cross section of our audiences knew and understood how to work social media, so participation numbers rose. Dance alumni started getting involved too, which was wonderful because they had experience performing in our concerts and could add valuable insights and questions into the conversation. I love this project because it's educational, but it meets students and young people where they live and pedagogically engages them through a format in which they feel comfortable.

This live social media experiment was on hold the past few years due to my sabbatical and the closing down of live performances. Interestingly, during Covid when we were forced to livestream our performances (which, post-Covid, we've kept doing alongside in-person shows), the combination of us posting information pertaining to each dance work and the viewers having a mechanism for response—the social media platform that we streamed through—we were able to keep some amount of educational discourse alive. I'm not sure if our audiences have come to expect this sort of communication from us and/or if they felt comfortable with the anonymity of the internet but, the engagement rate of the posts (the percentage of people who saw and interacted with the tweet) were higher than typical social media engagements for the college. Additionally, we discovered post-Covid via audience survey forms shared at intermission and after that show that this platform gave audience members a window into the creative process and engaged them in art in a new way. It made them feel part of the performance. Educating our audiences has strengthened our educational program, our attendance, and our community.

Notes

1 "Critical Response Process," Liz Lerman (website), accessed September 4, 2022, https://lizlerman.com/critical-response-process.
2 Daniel Nagrin, "'Rules' for Choreography: IN NO PARTICULAR ORDER," in *Choreography and the Specific Image* (Pittsburgh, PA: University of Pittsburgh Press, 2001), 59–75, accessed June 12, 2021, https://www.jstor.org/stable/j.ctt6wrbfq.9.

4

AUTHENTIC MOVEMENT

Figure 4.1 Student performance of authentic-inspired choreography.
Credit: ©Washington and Lee University, 2010.

DOI: 10.4324/9780367824167-5

AUTHENTIC MOVEMENT   59

I believe that authentic movement should be part of the choreographic process and has a prominent role in the choreographic flowchart, which appears in the next chapter. My definition of authentic movement should not be confused with Authentic Movement, which is a therapeutic practice associated with dance movement therapy where people express emotions or feelings through improvised movement.[1] Additionally, using the word *authentic* in this book is not a subjective value and should not be interpreted as a loaded term. To me, authentic movement means original, fresh movement that is similar to a codified technique in that it's painstakingly planned, worked, and edited but is different in that it is original to the creator. Stemming not from years of dance technique or study of someone else's form (although those could certainly be contributing factors), it is a unique creation. It is an essential component of composition and can lead to creative depth and exciting and distinct movements and styles of moving. Part of the reason I have become such a champion of authentic movement is that, over and over again, I've seen my college students for the past fifteen years, and younger dancers in the previous ten, use only the technique they've learned in class as their source material for creating a dance. They seemed unable to create original movements unless the vocabulary they were taught is the language of the entire dance.

In fact, as an assignment, I frequently ask my students to create a twenty-second dance, but the only rule is that it can only include movements for which there is no name. While they appear to understand the concept, after working alone for fifteen minutes, the first student's opening movement was a pas de bourrée. The rest of her piece included all named steps, as did the ballet, jazz, and gymnastics moves of the rest of the group. While the term "indoctrinated" isn't appropriate, I do feel that experienced dancers have studied for so long that the steps become one with their psyche, brain, bodies, and emotions. They seem unable to separate their technical skills from other ways of moving and seem mute without their trained physical language.

The difficulty of uncoupling from the technique is what I alluded to in Chapter 2 when I discussed "the burden of experience." My goal is that my composition course will help new choreographers not to part ways with their past training but to be aware of when they are borrowing from a dance tradition or training regimen, and learn how to use, edit, or configure those elements in a new way, and create from a place of pure ingenuity where they are speaking in their own voice. Interestingly, students that I've taught who have never taken a technique class often move uniquely and create compelling moments in space. It's almost as if intense training is an obstacle that either must be overcome or investigated so the dancer is always aware of choices she is making.

Because it is difficult for dancers to divorce themselves from their training, I have created "games" to help students get out of their heads and bodies and embrace new ways of moving without even realizing they are doing it. For me, cultivating authentic movement is an important skill for composition but also strengthens a dancer's overall proficiencies. After training in this methodology, what seems like a trick you play on your brain eventually becomes a natural process and a skill you can call on anytime. This aptitude also aids dancers in improvisation as both of these areas ask the dancer to move outside of traditional technique and create from a new place.

The following is a list of some of my dance games and accompanying explanations to aid movers in exploring authentic movement and shy away from relying on known techniques. I've placed them in order from least to most intellectually and/or kinesthetically challenging, although this order varies based on the experience and education of the students. You'll notice that some games require creating videos of the assignment and others are performed live. I tend to alternate between these two methods of expression (and sometimes, I use both).

Videoing assignments and showing them in class helps students who are new to dance, as they are typically shy about performing for their classmates. Videoing also gives them the time to mess up, fix things, and re-record, which is less stressful than the immediacy of having to do it once perfectly. Of course, doing it once perfectly is never part of the assignment or how I assess them. They place this pressure on themselves. It bears mentioning that, while I choose to use video for this purpose, it is a two-dimensional form that lacks the immediate dynamics of performance. A kinesthetic environment is lacking but I feel it's a small price to pay, initially, while students are insecure and looking for a safe place to create.

As the semester progresses, I incorporate live performance of the game assignments. This means they have to rehearse more on their own and commit the dance to memory in a more permanent way. I ensure that when discussing the product of these assignments in class, the students follow Liz Lerman's critical response process,[2] a feedback method that creates a safe zone for one another and encourages helpful responses that can be used for progression.

HAND DANCE

Directions: Using one hand or both hands and a flat surface, choreograph a thirty-second dance for the hand. Practice and perfect it. Video the dance and show the video in class.

Purpose: It's all but impossible to use dance technique on a hand. While you can make your fingers appear to be skipping or doing a split, for the most part, typical vocabulary is off the table.

Outcome: Generally, the students create a piece either on the floor or a table with the camera directly in front of the hand showing only from the wrist down to the surface. Occasionally, a student will take note of my broad directions and choose to video from a different angle, edit various angles/shots, use some sort of interesting background behind the hands, or somehow incorporate a prop, graphics, or lighting elements. Any of these approaches is fine but the important aspect of the assignment is to create a dance with movements that don't look anything like typical technique. I remind the students that if they can name a step to take it out. There are wonderful videos on YouTube of hand dances or "finger tutting" as expressed by the artists involved. One I enjoy showing is *Conceptual Dubstep Song* with Pnut's unique Finger Dance (Finger Tuts). The Dancer is also known as King Tutt.

Video reference 4.1

After all the student work has been shown, we watch a few of these pieces together as a class. Invariably the students are in awe of the breadth and depth of this creativity. They are made aware of the limitations they placed upon themselves and the depth of motions possible that they may not have considered. This is an important step forward. Recognizing our own limitations encourages us to look beyond what we already know and open up ourselves to new material.

RULES DANCE

Directions: Create a thirty-second dance in which you can only stand, sit, walk, and pause. Consider ways of moving, pathways, facings, and stage position. Practice and memorize for class shows.

Purpose: This assignment is very simple. It may seem counterintuitive given that my goal for these games is to pull dancers out of their training by not using named steps, however, my rules involve typical movements that all humans engage in, which for dancers can be difficult to transform into a dance as they are typically outside of the scope of their experience and training. This game is useful because it greatly limits the choices available to the student, enabling them to focus more deeply on what they can do creatively within those constraints.

Outcome: Because the steps are simple, students tend to be very innovative with *ways* of walking, sitting, and standing. Some engage their torso and allow it to lead the movement, others stand on one bent leg or their arms. They pay attention to where they are facing, diagonals, and the rhythm or style of their movement. They are able to delve deeply into these elements because the focus on *steps* has been taken away. This exercise creates a sensory experience that can be drawn upon later when working with more complex movements.

CUT-OUTS DANCE

Directions: Gather a group of magazines, newspapers, photos, or anything with an image that can be cut up. Cut out twelve shapes of anything that appeals to you with the exception of parts or the entirety of the human body. Glue the shapes, face side down, onto white paper, and then cut the paper around the shape following its edges exactly. We now have twelve cutouts with white paper on one side and the back side of the original image on the other. We sit in a circle on the floor, and I ask each student to organize the twelve shapes (with their white sides up) in a line from left to right in an order that appeals to them in

AUTHENTIC MOVEMENT   63

some way. The second part of this exercise varies each time I teach it but usually, the directions are something like this:

1. Choose the shape you dislike the most, and put it in the center of the circle. Reorder your shapes from left to right in a way that appeals to you.
2. Using the coin that I gave you, start at the leftmost shape and flip the coin. If you get heads, keep the shape. If you get tails, put the shape in the center of the circle. Once you've put four shapes into the center, stop flipping the coin. If you don't end up with four shapes in the center after having flipped the coin for all shapes, begin again from the start. Reorder the shapes from left to right in a way that appeals to you.
3. Starting with the student sitting to my right, choose the shape you like the most from the center pile, and give it to the person on your right. Reorder the shapes in a way that appeals to you.
4. Starting with the student sitting on my left, go around the circle one at a time, and steal one piece from any other student. Reorder the shapes in a way that appeals to you.
5. Starting with the student sitting directly across from me, choose a shape or shapes from the center, and give them to any other person. Keep adding pieces until their total number of shapes is ten. If they already have more than ten, remove whatever pieces you wish until they have ten. If they have ten shapes, trade two of their pieces with two of someone else's (or yours). Reorder their pieces from left to right in a way that appeals to you. They then repeat this with any other student. This pattern continues. A student may only interact with a student who hasn't already been chosen.
6. Everyone removes one shape and puts it in the center. Rotate half of your shapes into a new alignment, and reorder the shapes in a way that appeals to you.
7. Everyone stands up and moves two places to your right. The shapes in front of you will be used to create your dance. Using the shapes in their current order and orientation, create a nine-step dance. You may translate the shape onto your whole body, part of your body, as a pathway, or any other means. Be aware of the specifics of the shape as well as its overall bearing. You may add connective movements

so that you can flow from one movement to the other, but those moments may only serve as connections, not statements in their own right. Although we've been discussing shapes, the dance should be a phrase not a series of stop-action-like poses. Although the shapes are lying in a linear format on the floor, create your phrase in three dimensions being aware of facings, pathways, and stage space. The final dance should last no less than thirty seconds.

Purpose: The point of this exercise is to get dancers outside of their own heads, making shapes that have no bearing on their previous dance experience or steps.

Outcome: When students are asked to cut out images, they generally choose pictures that they like. I've seen a lot of martini glasses, wine bottles, and kittens, for example. To negate the natural tendency to make movements about the subject matter as opposed to the shape of the image, we glue the photos face down onto white paper. Once the image itself is removed, it's far easier to concentrate on the shape. We flip them over, white side up so that text or images on the opposite side don't infringe on the student's creativity. The copious steps are designed so that the students do not become attached to their pieces. There is some amount of chance involved with the coins and in allowing some students to choose pieces for others. This can result in biased decision-making where overly complex or other "disliked" shapes are ignored in favor of preferred shapes. The constant reordering of shapes usually creates a certain endearment by each student, and over time, they get attached to their palette. For this reason, the final step draws loud groans from the entire crowd.

HIDDEN CAMERA DANCE

Directions: Using your iPhone or camera, video one or more of your professors lecturing. (Be sure to ask permission first.) This can also be done by accumulating footage while people-watching, walking around town, in a restaurant, library, etc. (although be aware of permissions/ privacy). Video them off and on over two class periods or two days.

Create a thirty-second piece that transposes their gestures and mannerisms into a dance. Show the edited version of the video in class and perform the dance inspired by it.

Purpose: Give the students experience with pedestrian movement and gestures and the challenge that comes with transposing them into dance phrases. Limit the students to non-dance movements so they focus on shape-making not "steps."

Outcome: This exercise tends to be very difficult for the students mainly because their footage is filled only with gesticulations and sometimes walking and sitting. There's not a lot of material, and most of it is fairly reserved so the leap to making phrases is a bit more challenging. Elements of effort, force, and time come into play and force the students to incorporate more than just shape-making into their projects.

PROP DANCE

Directions: Choose a prop to be your partner in a one-minute dance. The prop needs to be large enough to dance in, on, and around but small enough to be transportable. You must be in contact with the object in some way for the entire dance, and your movement choices must be based on the shape of the prop and transitioning from one interaction to the other. Perform your dance with the prop for the class.

Purpose: Using a prop as inspiration for a dance engages the students in determining how to interact and shape a dance around the edges, curves, size, and weight of an inanimate object. Interacting with the object becomes source material for the phraseology.

Outcome: I edit and re-edit my directions for clarity because there are always some students who put a teddy bear, a rolling chair, or an umbrella on the stage and dance around it. Also, the tendency for using the object for its intended purpose only (sitting on the chair) is high. I encourage the students to use the object for anything other than its intended purpose, feel its weight and height, and allow it to hold them, if possible. I demonstrate molding the body to the shape of the object and choosing to move based solely on manipulating the prop. There have been times when we've repeated this exercise for the group to fully explore it.

66 AUTHENTIC MOVEMENT

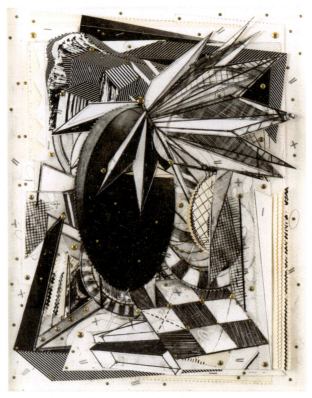

Figure 4.2 U1992.13.1, *Collage, Tree for Mine*, Robert James Reed, mixed media, 1991. Credit: Courtesy of Museums at Washington and Lee University, Lexington, Virginia.

ART INSPIRATION DANCE

Directions: Choose an artwork from anywhere on campus as inspiration, and create a one-minute, thirty-second dance that reflects the style of the painting. This can be tied to color, hue, contrast, brush strokes, line, design, composition style, or any other graphic element. The piece should reference the artwork and draw inspiration from it but shouldn't recreate, record, or document any part of the original source. Do not incorporate a story or interpretation of the meaning of the painting in this dance. (This can certainly be done with sculpture and other artworks as well.) In class, project the painting onto the wall and dance in front of it.

Purpose: To challenge the students to experiment with inspiration and how to deal with creating something new without copying or parroting the original and also tying the movement to concrete aspects of the artwork. To give students the opportunity to learn to speak about visual art and how it relates to movement.

Outcome: This is a fun exercise in which the students reflect on a work of art. (It's also a great way to introduce them to the campus art archives and become familiar with the art hanging on campus.) The students tend to be confident in this exercise because they are interpreting onto their bodies the strokes of the paintings. I added into my directions the caveat that students should not interpret the meaning of the paintings because, originally, that was all the students performed. I want this assignment to specifically address the strokes and style used, not the subject matter because I felt there was too much room for interpretation when dealing only with thematic material. I want to encourage students to deal with more concrete and measurable outcomes.

MOTION CAPTURE DANCE

Directions: Using motion capture equipment and a motion capture suit, improvise throughout the space and gather four to five minutes of material. Download the footage and, using iMovie, edit the portions of the phrases that appeal to you. Use the program to cut out portions that you don't wish to use, reverse, speed up, slow down, and edit together at least one minute of movement. Learn the one-minute movement phrase. Show the original motion capture edits and then perform it for the class.

Purpose: This is an initial exercise as part of a larger effort to train students to edit movement in a tangible way. They will then use these skills later for composition.

Outcome: Students love this exercise because they can see their motion capture avatar on the television while they are moving and can edit, change, and switch up movements in real-time as they are being recorded. They move freely and refrain from focusing on individual movements because they understand that it will all be edited later. It is quite freeing for them and gets them out of their heads.

WEB DANCE

Directions: Using YouTube, DVDs, Jacob's Pillow website, TikTok, or other sources, choose a dance that appeals to you in some way, and teach yourself a thirty-second excerpt from it. (Length can be adjusted based on the difficulty of the phrase.) Rehearse and video the excerpt. Next, create a thirty-second phrase that was inspired by this piece but does not contain any of the choreography performed in the same way as the original. You may abstract the movement, put it on a new part of the body, dance it in reverse, and change pathways, stage directions, facings, or axes, for example. The goal is to show the connection and inspiration but see two different dances. In class, show the original dance, then show your videoed version of that dance, and perform the abstracted version live.

Purpose: To challenge the students to experiment with inspiration and how to deal with creating something new without copying or parroting the original. This exercise is challenging because the inspiration source is dance, therefore, the urge to duplicate movements will be strong.

Outcome: This exercise is usually done toward the end of the term when the technique is blended with authentic movement to create choreography that is original and specific to the individual. Learning how to take inspiration from something without recreating it but including abstracted or other elements that tie back to the original is an exercise in creative problem solving. It also opens up the class for a larger discussion of copyright. This exercise is challenging because the students feel caught between reflecting on the work and creating something new, and they have difficulty discerning imitation from the impression. This is an opportunity to introduce concepts of inspiration verses appropriation.

IMPROV DANCE

Directions: Move throughout the space for twenty minutes, feeling the air and architecture around you and your body moving in space and time. Explore your body in its surroundings. Videotape yourself improvising for five to eight minutes after this. Using iMovie, edit your footage to include movements that appeal to you. Reorder, and change timing, directions, and sequence of movements to create a phrase that appeals to you in some way. The final product must be at least two minutes. Show the original video and then perform the dance.

Purpose: To begin to incorporate authentic movement back into the dance vocabularies of the students. Allow them the freedom to move with no pressure, knowing that footage will be edited later. Teach them how to use iMovie as a source for composition.

Outcome: Some students are initially quite timid about moving freely in space with no guidance. I require the initial twenty minutes of them moving as a group so that they can free themselves of overthinking what they are doing and relieve any pressure of "performing." They seem to achieve a sort of Zen state eventually so that when the video recording begins, they are mentally in a place to accept it and contribute to the assignment. They seem to like having the authority to pick and choose what works for them via the editing software and tangibly being able to move dance components around to create their dance.

CHANCE DANCE

Directions: Using the resulting movement combination or final phrases from the above games, use a die to determine which movements you will use and the order in which they will occur. First, assign heads on a coin to "keep" and tails to "leave." Starting at the first dance game, flip the coin. Make a note of "keep" or "leave." Continue this way through all nine dance games. Then using whatever games have been "kept," begin again, and repeat the coin flipping with just those games. Continue repeating this way until only two games are left. Next, break up the phrasing from the first game into six parts and assign a number to each portion. The way in which the phrasing is broken up/length of each piece is at the discretion of the maker. Roll the die four times. The number rolled each of the four times corresponds to the phrase with that number. So, for example, if on your first roll, you roll a five, then the fifth phrase goes first. On the next roll, if you roll a one, then the first phrase goes second.

70   AUTHENTIC MOVEMENT

> Do this four times so that the new resulting phrase is made up of four rolls/phrases. (The same number can be rolled/assigned twice.) Finally, break up the phrase from the second game into ten parts of the makers' choosing. Roll the dice ten times. If the number is between one and three, you keep the phrase. If it is between four and six, you do not use the phrase. Continue with this throughout all ten sections. At the end of rolling the die, if you have zero or ten parts, repeat the process. Ideally, you are left with four to eight sections. Put the first and second phrases together in that order. Learn and rehearse. In class, show the original two phrases via video and then perform the chance phrase live. The final product should be no less than two minutes.
>
> **Purpose:** Using existing movements, create phrases that are ordered by chance. Take away decision making from the creator to reveal creative combinations that may not have otherwise been considered. This is an opportunity to talk about Merce Cunningham and John Cage's use of chance in their work.
>
> **Outcome:** This assignment piggybacks on and creatively combines the phraseology from the student's previous work. They learn to accept (although most don't like) that the power of making choices has been taken from them. This exercise includes multiple movements that, when put together, resemble phrases, and *feel* like choreography.

In all these examples, I'm working toward pushing the students out of their comfort zones. It's easy for them to rely on the vocabulary that they've been taught prior to college, but that material could be outdated, limited, or highly specific to a particular person, technique, or style. Put another way, most students have only experienced one particular school or individual's approach and therefore were given limited resources. Pushing the ballet student to experience dancing with, under, and around a prop or the hip hop dancer to experience shapes inspired by photos provides those students with information relating to movement options for a specific assignment and opens up their artist's eye to an entirely new process and a new way of moving.

Part of the reason there are so many options in this game phase is because, initially, most students resist these new avenues. They've been taught that the way they move is the only legitimate approach, and their hesitation stems from insecurity and a fear of trying something new or challenging. Making yourself vulnerable to a professor and a studio full of other dancers/students is daunting but when I teach composition, my pedagogical approach is to assume nothing and start everyone from square one.

Of course, a large part of this philosophy is understanding that my role as a professor is to create a space where they feel comfortable and safe sharing themselves. This includes a space where they are working together as a community to move forward, a space that values critical response in a positive, wholistic, and gentle way, a space that includes me also making myself vulnerable so that they see the importance of working openly, bravely, and for the betterment of one other and the art form.

Digital Media as a Tool for Authentic Movement

Though mentioned briefly earlier as part of the dance games, I'd like to take a moment to discuss how digital video editing software can be a wonderful partner in composing. Whether your favorite editing software is iMovie, Final Cut Pro, Elements, or any of the countless other options,

Figure 4.3 Motion capture of student dancer, IQ Center.
Credit: ©Washington and Lee University, 2016.

I've had pedagogical success using them to help students assess their movement phrases and improvisation, edit their work, and help them organize their phrases as I will outline below.

One of the frustrations of new choreographers is not being able to *see* their work. Some of them create phrases on their own bodies, take notes, and maybe even video themselves but feel disheartened when they wish to alter the sequence of movements or phrases, try something backward or from a different angle, or want to see options side by side before making decisions one way or the other. When creating solos and without dancers to set work on, it's easy to feel discouraged or, out of irritation at the process, to take a simple path that does not involve rich, complex movement.

To combat this issue and to provide students with a support mechanism, I use iMovie as a choreography tool. I think it's the simplest and most user-friendly of the options (perhaps also the cheapest), and it ensures that students are up and working quickly. I've found that most students today are already experienced to some degree in iMovie. For those who do not have a Mac, I check out iPads from the library for their use. I explain how to upload the video to iMovie from a phone or camera, edit and organize clips in the timeline viewer, and trim unwanted portions. I show them how to change the speed of a clip or portion of a clip, reverse the clip, rotate it, flip the image, and include transitions. These options give the students a place to start that feels familiar. Almost every student has a connection to digital media in some form, so pairing this place of comfort with what they usually view as an intimidating choreographic process provides them with a comfortable place from which to experiment.

Other digital tools that are a bit more limiting but nevertheless helpful are movement generators. *Dancemaker*, created by 92Y Dance Education Library and 92Y Harkness Dance Center, offers word choices in the Laban categories of Body, Effort, Space, and Relationship to aid students in exploring the breadth and depth of choices. It tracks and compiles your choices and allows you to view your dance in words, which is helpful for memorization and storage purposes. It begins with a "word cloud," which is a lengthy list of words from which you can choose, or you can select "theme" to be shown a list of words that relate specifically to the theme you've chosen. It then takes you to a new page where the word you chose is applied to body, effort, space, and relationship, and more word options are presented under each category. You can repeat this process from the beginning to add more words

AUTHENTIC MOVEMENT   73

to your dance. When finished, the app will print your dance in words to give you a script from which to begin to move.

DanceForms2 is a helpful tool as well. It uses 3D animation so that the choreographer is seeing bodies move in space. It offers the creator single dancers or group ensembles to pose and shape and has the power to play back choreography and let you edit/manipulate the footage. This program is not practical for an introductory-level composition class because it assumes the user has knowledge of dance terms, biomechanics, and kinesiology. It's quite comprehensive and takes time to learn. It may work best for a yearlong class where time isn't so compressed.

Both *Dancemaker* and *DanceForms2* have pre-existing vocabularies in libraries, which, though helpful, may inhibit the authentic movement roots that I'm working to establish in new choreographers. For these reasons, I prefer using iMovie as it is a simple solution that doesn't feed the student's options and gives them the freedom to digitally edit sequences, organize them, and alter the order of movements very simply. Obviously, iMovie doesn't support the creation of new movements, but iPhone or other video sources can document improvisations, trials, and rehearsals for later editing via iMovie. Ultimately, iMovie allows for the review, editing, and sequencing of movement on video that can later be translated back onto the body.

I have a dance game using *Dancemaker* that, although the app limits you to certain words, gives the students a lot of experience working with Laban Movement Analysis, which comprises a large part of our choreographic flowchart.

APP DANCE

Directions: Download the DEL Dancemaker app. Click the "Create New" box on the bottom right. Choose ten words from the master list, ten words within whatever theme you wish ("Theme" is on the top right) or click the typewriter in the bottom right corner to type in your own words. Click Next. Choose one option under Body, Effort, Space, and Relationship that you wish to dance. Click the right arrow to move to the second word. Repeat this process for all ten words. Click View Dance to see the list of words and corresponding movement information you've

> chosen. Screenshot the dance you made. Use this script to make a one-minute dance. Video your dance and upload it to the class site.
>
> **Purpose:** To gain experience with Laban principles and the basic Eight Effort Elements so that those principles can be applied to other projects. Practice making a dance with a finite source of words and LMA principles.
>
> **Outcomes:** The students tend to like this exercise because using technology is familiar and, because the vocabulary and structure for the dance exist, it gives them a jumping-off point. This is an accessible and effective exercise for the start of the semester because it supports new choreographers as it guides them through the process of making something original.

I am fortunate to have access to the IQ lab at my college and to my brilliant colleague, Dave Pfaff, who is an academic technologist and in charge of the space. The Integrative and Quantitative Center is a collaborative space that contains state-of-the-art technology to aid with teaching and learning. For the past few years, I've worked with Dave and his staff using motion capture to aid with new and authentic movement development. Over the years we've experimented with downloading and editing motion capture for use in composition and with printing 3D models of captured movement,

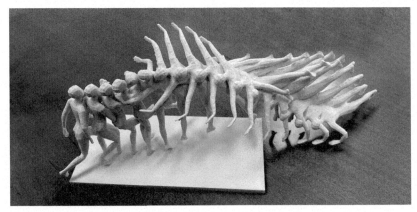

Figure 4.4 3D printing of a student dancer jumping and landing.
Credit: ©Washington and Lee University 2022.

AUTHENTIC MOVEMENT   75

and we've danced with ourselves in virtual reality. It's inventive and inspiring and enables the dancers to see and process movement in a new way. Pedagogically, it provides the students with unconventional options for seeing and moving that encourage them to think about and generate movement in new ways. This experiential learning methodology is described below:

Experiments in Motion Capture in Dance, by Dave Pfaff

David Pfaff is an academic technologist in the Integrative and Quantitative Center at Washington and Lee University (IQ Center). He helps faculty find innovative ways to integrate a wide range of technology into their classes and research. The IQ Center houses an array of technologies including 3D printing, laser cutting, microscopy, photography, reality capture, high-speed imaging, motion capture, virtual and augmented reality as well as computers and software. The mission of the center is to make these technologies easily accessible to the widest audience on campus.

Unlike a video camera that records a scene from a fixed vantage point, motion capture systems track and record complete three-dimensional positions of people and objects. Data collected via motion capture systems can be used to simply make measurements or in more creative ways. For example, data is often used to give motion to computer-generated characters in movies and games. Applied to dance, motion capture applications can range from the analytical to the abstract.

The process begins by attaching reflective markers to a dancer's body. Depending on the detail required, the number of markers can range from just a couple to a set of fifty or more. For example, tracking individual fingers requires more markers than tracking hands alone. During capture, the position of the markers is determined by special cameras placed around the room. Other systems use self-contained sensors to measure movement without the need for cameras. In all cases, computers record the position data while dancers perform.

Over the past few years our lab—the Integrative and Quantitative Center (IQ Center)—has collaborated with dance faculty to explore creative ways to use motion capture data to craft experiences for dance students. The first time we incorporated motion capture into a dance assignment, only the position of the hands was tracked. Students then used 3D design software to create a digital sculpture from the paths of their hands. Markers were placed along the paths at a fixed time interval to indicate the speed of the hands along the path. Once complete, we 3D printed the finished sculptures.

In another more complex assignment, full-body motion capture data was applied to computer-generated characters and inserted into a virtual reality (VR) system. Students could then wear a VR headset and interact with a life-size avatar of their own dance compositions. In the virtual world, students were able to control the speed of the playback and add streamers that would provide a persistent visual trace of the path of the hands. The VR system also allowed students to move anywhere in the virtual space to examine the dance from any vantage point.

Figure 4.5 3D printing of a student dancer doing floorwork.
Credit: Courtesy of Misha Lin, 2022.

Motion capture data can also be used to render artistic, fantastical versions of the original dance composition. We recently used motion graphics software to add particle systems, water, hair, and even fire simulations to the motion capture data. In some cases, the underlying dance movement was almost completely obscured by the added elements, but the results were visually striking.

The variety of applications makes motion capture a powerful tool for dance. Unlike video recording, a motion capture system allows users to decide later how the data is used, and the options are limitless.

Notes

1 Patrizia Pallaro (Ed.). *Authentic Movement: Essays by Mary Starks Whitehouse, Janet Adler, and Joan Chodorow*. London, England: Jessica Kingsley Publishers, 1999.
2 "Critical Response Process," Liz Lerman (website), accessed September 4, 2022, https://lizlerman.com/critical-response-process

5

CHOREOGRAPHIC FLOWCHART

Figure 5.1 M(other).
Credit: ©Washington and Lee University 2016.

DOI: 10.4324/9780367824167-6

CHOREOGRAPHIC FLOWCHART   79

Dance composition must battle against the belief that creativity is something you are imbued with from birth or a mystical, magical gift that is bestowed upon the deserving. Talent, too, is a loaded word because it presupposes the same. These words imply that dance is birthed fully formed from the brain of a "chosen one." By using this language, one removes all of the rigor inherent in making art. This does an injustice to the artmaker as it removes the truth of the process: the trial, experimentation, editing, discarding, reimagining, refinement, and countless other stages in the creation and development of the piece. This way of thinking strips the artist of the true cost of the labor involved in creation.

Ironically, this "heavenly bestowed" way of looking at art can also cause people to view critically anything that they feel isn't rigorous or beautiful *enough*. Thirty-two fouettés are impossible for the average person but if anyone can paint a square canvas blue, where is the value? In this case, one may feel the artist doesn't have God-given talent, therefore, the value of what they create is reduced. This logic implies that virtuosity, in and of itself, has value, an idea that further erodes the truth in artistry.

I see in my students an insecurity about whether they have "what it takes" to make art. The general consensus that only the chosen few can make art is so ingrained in their experience, they are paralyzed by it. They feel that they haven't experienced a light from above, an out-of-body experience, water turning into wine, or a burning bush, so who are they to create anything? (And for the record, in my opinion, "what it takes" is tenacity, dedication, bravery, patience, faith, humility, and stubbornness, to name a few. Knowledge gained from studying how to make dance. Sweat and tears. Blinding fear. Work. Not missives from heavenly hosts seated at the right hand of God.)

While many wonderful composition books have been written to aid young choreographers, during my many years of teaching composition, I felt a need for scaffolding of sorts to support the choreographic process. My students needed something tangible as a foundation while they coped with the intangibilities of movement, time, and space. Composition traditionally is not taught as a process or organized system. Its customary lack of structure proves daunting to those approaching it for the first time.

Thus, over a number of years, I created, worked, and edited a composition flowchart (and eventually made a companion) to help my students when they were floundering. I felt it somewhat dangerous to have this flowchart out in the world because its very existence suggests that dances are constructed from beginning to end or through some format that, if you only follow the directions, will result in a work of art. My fear was that their takeaway from this chart would be a mechanized view that assumes that if you input movement into door one, for example, a finished work of art will be deposited out of door twelve. I found, however, over the years, that if I created a flexible structure with many options, footnotes, and freedoms, and no right or wrong way to approach it, students at least have something to grasp ahold of when working with intangibles and ephemerals of shaping time and space. Some students use this as a set of training wheels just until they get their bearings, and others continue with it as a tangible reminder of what should be present when considering, playing, researching, and developing new work.

As with much of this book, this process is based on my experience teaching dancers how to sculpt bodies in space. I don't claim that it's a miracle solution to choreography nor do I claim all of its components to be my own. I have pieced together this chart from bits of information that spoke to me from twenty years of composition textbooks that I've used in class, from thirty years of viewing and responding to student and professional dance, and from my own personal choreography experiences.

A key theoretical foundation underlying this chart is Laban/Bartenieff Movement Analysis, which beautifully outlines "a method and a language for describing, visualizing, interpreting, and documenting all varieties of human movement."[1] This flowchart is meant simply to serve as a roadmap but one without rigid directions. It helps the choreographer down a path but doesn't dictate how to proceed or where to turn. It's a framework for new choreographers to give them the courage to begin. I will include the flowchart first descriptively in outline form and later pictorially and define each element that I touch on. When I arrive at Laban/Bartenieff fundamentals, I will not go into too much detail as I don't wish to claim their work or recreate or repeat something that is available so plentifully elsewhere.

After the description of each portion of the flowchart and the graphic that sums it up, I will include a second, alternative flowchart that I completed after the original. The first flowchart was made with young choreographers in mind. (By "young," I mean new to choreography. Young choreographers can be any age.) I approached the model using writing as a metaphor and set it up with terms like "theme" and "development" and the understanding of a "topic sentence" so that anyone who understands grammar would feel comfortable. Later, I created a second model, based on the same ideas and containing all the same elements of the original but the order of things and, in some cases, the names of steps, have been altered to fit within a model that is suited to visual and performing artists. (After creating these models, I decided that a wonderful assignment for an advanced composition class would be to task the students with making their own personal flowchart that organizes and describes dance in a way that speaks to them and their process, and challenges them to relate their choreographic style and process to their diagram. This would be an exciting assignment to review!) I will go into a little detail at the end to tie the original and revamped models together so that the overarching goals are clear.

The first two steps of the flowchart are inspired by Jacqueline Smith-Autard's *Dance Composition: A Practical Guide to Creative Success in Dance Making*.[2] I used her basic ideas as a jumping-off point and organized them in a way that made sense to me. I added elements that I feel are important and clarified descriptions for my own purposes. (Note: there are many places in these flowcharts where, after the last example, I include "etc." This means that I've given a few examples but there are many others. I've simply outlined a jumping-off point. No student should feel that what I've listed are the only options. Limitless possibilities exist, and I encourage the reader to explore and find more examples.)

I. Concept

A. *Stimulus*

That thing that stirs you, that engages your mind and/or spirit, that heightens your senses, or evokes a reaction. The spark that leads you to inspiration. This can serve as the starting place for your dance, but it doesn't have to. Many times, you may think you're making a dance about inspiration XYZ but after working, researching, and following where the work leads, you may find you're actually exploring something quite different. You may, for example, become fascinated with a certain aspect of the original stimulus that moves you tangentially away from what you planned. Or you may find that the original stimulus can be distilled down to something else. Many times, when you open yourself up to see where the process leads, it will show you something you'd never have anticipated. Try not to feel tied to your stimulus. Allow it to evolve, grow, and develop in whatever way it needs to. A stimulus can adjust just like any other aspect of this flowchart. Don't feel trapped.

1. sight
2. sound
3. movement
4. touch
5. smell
6. idea, etc.

B. Inspiration

What the stimulus incites, brings to mind, or makes you feel or think. The ignition of your desire to investigate or explore. For example, if your stimulus is the feeling of community at your local coffee shop, you may be inspired to begin research on coffee culture and its origins in seventeenth-century Paris.

1. Type: Answers the question, *What* are you communicating? Through what method do you want to express your inspiration? What will you use to create an account of events/plot/your expression? There doesn't only have to be one answer here. This can be an amalgam of things.

   a. story/narrative
   b. theme
   c. comedy
   d. drama
   e. biography/autobiography
   f. clear/kinesthetics, etc.

2. Method: Answers the question, *How* are you communicating? What are the means through which you will present your piece? How do you want to express your inspiration? What format will you use to speak? I list five points on a spectrum here. There is gray area between all of these points and more on either side of the continuum. No one of these is expected to carry the weight of an entire dance alone, although it could. There is a lot of potential for creativity when they work in tandem with one another, play with, and riff off each other. Because the definitions may be a little opaque, I've included in italics a simple example. Each example is based on the premise that you wish to include "stop" in your piece. I've listed one example for each method of presentation in italics.

   a. Clear: Representing nothing, without connotations, devoid of influence, having no specific meaning, authentic, movement purely about moving, kinesthetics. *You wouldn't necessarily use this device if you wanted a specific image or idea because the clear movement does not represent anything specific. It is a movement for the sake of movement. Therefore, there is no stop sign example.*

   b. Abstract: A contrived ordering, obscuring the appearance of something specific so that it is hidden or difficult to see or interpret, separated from reality.[3] *The dancer, facing stage left, completes a series of torso undulations. She turns to face the audience and freezes, holds that freeze for an uncomfortable amount of time, then turns backstage left as she begins moving again.*

   c. Symbolic: Associated meanings that are independent of an object or subject, representing something else, relating to something else but not completely obscured, extracting part of the essence, and adding other features.[4] *Standing still in center stage looking out at the audience with right arm raised to shoulder height, flexed elbow in traditional "stop" pose, and holding a red helium balloon.*

   d. Representational: Depicting something in its actual state, standing for something else but closely linked to reality. *A dancer walks onstage holding a painting of a stop sign.*[5]

   e. Literal: Gesture, representing the exact thing with no variation, truth. *The dancer walks onstage holding a stop sign.*

C. Research

What will you do with your inspiration, the ideas you've generated from it, and your plans for how you will express and present them? What needs to happen with the kernel of your idea so that it blossoms and grows? Employing a variety of these methods in researching your idea/inspiration will ground the work, create opportunities for growth and development, and lead you down new paths. Once work begins it should follow a repeated triangular pattern of:

Figure 5.2 Research triangle.
Credit: Davies, 2022.

For example, say you are inspired by a field of poppies. Through your research method *trial*, you create a journal that includes photos, drawings, and paintings of poppies as well as text from research on how they grow and what makes them thrive. As you develop your ideas, you may *select* photos and elements of paintings only, and edit out drawings. You then *focus* on the photos and paintings and decide that what appeals to you most are the orange and red images, so you *refine* to include those colors only. Then you sweep back to *trial* and begin again with a more defined path and circle again, each time editing down and/or opening up to new selections. You may have forgotten about the research involving growing methods and climates from earlier, so you focus on it more deeply this time around. You may select the number associated with the growing zone in which they thrive or the length of time they flower. Maybe you later refine these numbers and decide you will use their shapes as pathways on the floor within your piece, or you assign movement shapes that look like those numbers as part of the phrasing. This process repeats, and your research grows and develops, leading you down new paths for further exploration. In some cases, these pieces of the puzzle may not be associated or have any sort of recognizable affiliation. It may be also that your research alters what

CHOREOGRAPHIC FLOWCHART   85

you initially intended for type and method of presentation, and you need to go back to those elements and rearrange/rethink them. Many times, throughout your use of this flowchart, your current choices will reflect previous ones. That's good. The piece will begin to take shape and, at any point along the way, something within may send ripples forward and backward along the path. As you begin to move through the process and into movement, the points may change even again. That's fine too. Try to let the process unfurl in its own way.

1. drawing
2. research
3. interviews
4. observation
5. journaling
6. drawing
7. improvisation, etc.

II. Practice

A. Structure

The configuration, the overall shape of the piece. This can be as general or specific as you wish, and it can change as the work develops.

1. solo
2. duet
3. one large group work
4. trio in three movements
5. fifteen-member ensemble in five movements, etc.

B. Theme

The basic idea, the synthesis or initial motivation, your topic sentence, and the foundation. Used to guide the process and motivate the work. This can be words, movements, a combination of the two, or anything that will serve as the guiding principle that moves the piece forward. As with any of the stages of this flowchart, this can change. As one moving piece alters, an ensuing change shifts and transforms other aspects of the work. The piece is living, so try not to strangle it or dictate where it should go.

C. Development

The arrangement, the internal structure, the heart of the piece. This is where the majority of the movement experience lives. This area ties movement with meaning and expression. This is the process through which a choreographer articulates his/her/their feelings, emotions, story, etc., and makes choices to communicate and convey their movement voice to the audience. This entire section references the fundamentals of Laban Movement Analysis/Bartenieff Fundamentals (LMA/BF). This entire system is quite deep and comprehensive. The four major categories can be divided and subdivided in detail and cover much more material than is indicated here. However, because this is just one facet of the larger flowchart, we use LMA/BF in its simplest form. There are many places online where the full LMA/BF is documented and described. I advise researching on your own for the full version.

Rudolph Laban, a pioneer of modern dance in Europe, invented a system of dance analysis and notation in the early twentieth century. He sought to give language to movement and categorize human motion, so he developed a system that analyzes movement in three-dimensional space and divides it into categories of body, effort, shape, and space. Each of these categories breaks down further to define and clarify the classification of integrated elements.[6] Irmgard Bartenieff was Laban's student and protégé. Her research as a physical therapist and in nonverbal behavior led her to expound upon Laban's work by integrating physical reeducation and total body connectivity to his guiding principles.[7]

1. Body: Answers the question, What?, action, the way in which the body moves.

    a. jump, bend, twist, stillness, jumping, turning, leaping, etc.

CHOREOGRAPHIC FLOWCHART   87

2. Effort: Answers the question, How?, the quality of the movement, how the body moves.

    a. space

        i. direct

        ii. indirect

    b. weight

        i. strong

        ii. light

    c. time

        i. sustained

        ii. sudden

    d. flow

        i. free

        ii. bound

The first three items contained in this Effort portion make up what is known as Laban's "Efforts of Action Drive."[8] By combining one of each element listed under space, weight, and time, we have the eight basic elements. Laban claims that one or more of these movement qualities is present, in some degree, in every possible motion. By combining them in different ways, the

EIGHT EFFORTS GRAPH

SPACE	WEIGHT	TIME	EFFORT	EXAMPLE
Direct	Strong	Sudden	Punch	Punch / jump / stamp
Direct	Strong	Sustained	Press	Pushing a heavy piece of furniture across a carpet / press a hamburger flat / squeezing
Direct	Light	Sudden	Dab	Painting dots with a paint brush / typing / dab alcohol on a cut
Direct	Light	Sustained	Glide	Roller skating / Ice skating
Indirect	Strong	Sudden	Slash	Swinging a sword / swinging a tennis racket/ whip
Indirect	Strong	Sustained	Wring	Squeeze water out of a washcloth / twisting
Indirect	Light	Sudden	Flick	Flicking an insect off of your face / flick cigarette butt out the window
Indirect	Light	Sustained	Float	A helium balloon / floating on your back in water / weightlessness

Figure 5.3 Eight efforts graph.

Credit: Davies' rendition of one of the numerous graphs created by Laban and others depicting the same.

dancer can express words, thoughts, and feelings, through movement.[9] A configuration incorporating flow is described as "Full Effort Actions".[10]

3. Space: Answers the question, Where?, the environment, the Kinesphere in which you are moving.

   a. levels

      i. high
      ii. low, etc.

   b. shape

      i. curved
      ii. straight, etc.

   c. direction

      i. upstage
      ii. stage right, etc.

   d. planes

      i. sagittal
      ii. peripheral
      iii. transverse
      iv. frontal, etc.

4. Shape: Answers the question, With whom or what?, the relationship between the bodies to one another and to the environment.

   a. canon/unison
   b. mirror/copy
   c. adding/substituting
   d. symmetric/asymmetric
   e. repetition
   f. contrasting/same
   g. juxtaposition, etc.

To ensure that movements are being chosen to underline, express and/or reflect the inspiration, we move from the bottom of the chart back to the top. We move from the body, effort, space, and shape back to inspiration, to research, to theme. Individual components wind their way through the flowchart and float back up to the top as they are edited and effect other systems. In this way, trial, refinement, and selection happen over and over again bouncing between elements of concept and elements of production. They may follow different paths. For example, shape elements may change based on new discoveries in movement research, but those discoveries may not affect effort so that might remain the same. Or the body may offer new material if the source of inspiration yields additional ideas, but the type and method may not need to be changed. The close relationship of these elements and their interdependence and also independence is imperative as the development of the material refers to the inspiration and theme in order to tell its story.

This process is always ongoing, developing, and changing throughout the creation of the choreography. You may go through the entire flowchart and end with one sixteen-count phrase, or you may have five minutes of material. The chart may be used simply as a jumping-off point, or it can guide you through your entire piece. As the dance begins to reveal itself, there may be certain elements of the chart that are more helpful than others. Only use what you need. There is no right or wrong way to do it.

D. Your toolbox

As mentioned previously, for most students, creative writing language helps to simplify concepts surrounding theme, development, and editing of thematic material, but when I speak about refining and editing choreography, I use studio art vocabulary. I talk about shading and highlighting, the density of color and light brush strokes, rules of threes, and asymmetry, among others. Many studio art terms also imply nuance, which suggests subtlety, a wonderfully specific delicacy that is all too often forgotten in dance composition.

As a means of organization and to facilitate class discussion, I arranged into two subcategories devices or "tools" to aid in composition: *tools of internal structure* and *tools of external structure*. By internal structure, I mean that the devices don't need more than one person to be useable. For example, in order to use mirroring, you need someone else on the stage. Similarly, one person must have another in the space in order to imitate, oppose, or

Figure 5.4 Davies working with a student dancer.
Credit: ©Washington and Lee University 2019.

follow their movements. Using a literal tool as an example, a screwdriver has no use without a screw. Vice versa is true. They are dependent on one another. In addition to pairs, some choreographic tools need a group of dancers to explore. A canon, for example, requires more than two people to generate a sense of ordered sequencing.

I also look to internal tools as methodology to bend and shape the structure of one dancer and the internal meaning within one body. These tools relate specifically to the relationship of one body part to another, of one body in space, of one body in time. It's important to note that all of the solo tools can be used in groups as well, but the group tools generally need two or more dancers in order for them to be recognized as such. Having said this, there are no rules, and there are always creative ways to circumvent definitive statements. That's part of what makes choreography fascinating.

It may be, for example, that a choreographer wishes to create a canon and set it on a soloist where the one person dances an excerpt of part of a canon, or the canon is compressed so one person can do both parts, or through some other creative method. This may not be a recognizable canon but one which has been employed nonetheless. I think of the external tools as devices that helps to shape space and time between and within two or more dancers. In order to have asymmetry on stage, it's necessary to have a group so that they can be arranged throughout the space in a way that is unbalanced to the eye.

Again, I hesitate to give anyone the impression that these are inflexible definitions. I may wish to move a soloist around the stage in such a way that I place her in ten different positions on the stage and create a scenario wherein if she had been ten dancers, the space would have been imbalanced. I may choose to suspend time by allowing her to assume all ten roles in an asynchronous time flow. However, to provide clarity for young choreographers, I categorize these tools assuming we'd like them to be visible as such. In the paragraphs below, I give some examples of each of these categories. They are by no means complete nor must they be permanently situated where I've put them. All of this is open to conversation and debate.

1. *Tools of internal structure* consist of a framework with seemingly endless opportunities for creative variations and arrangement. Placement, facing, sequencing, order, accumulation, rewinding, cutting, and pasting all refer to the ways in which the material is conceived, assembled, ordered, and set on a dancer. All of these tools can be used on soloists or groups of dancers.

Directional *facings* of the dancers and where they are positioned on stage can nonverbally communicate strength or weakness, boldness or shyness, intimacy, candidness, truth, etc. For example, if nine dancers are facing upstage right and one is downstage staring at the audience, one might feel a defiance or a power in the single dancer. Similarly, if all the dancers are huddled into a corner, one might infer fear or cowering or maybe something less symbolic and more representational like a flock of birds huddling in the rain.

In much the same way, *levels* are used to forward the communicative power of movements and phrases as well as helping to design the space.

A dancer that repeats a thirty-two-count phrase from the first section of the dance but performs it lying down instead of standing up immediately raises questions. A viewer may remember the phrase from earlier and immediately see that a choice was made to repeat it in a prone position. What does it mean that the composer chose to repeat or to cut and paste this phrase but clearly show it from a new angle, with more space around it, and from a new perspective? These choices are clues and share in the informative power of the piece.

Tools of *placement*, position, and movement texture give the audience clues. They have communicative power. What does it mean when ten women form a circle all facing into one another on center stage? What images does that conjure? Witches around a cauldron? Athletes before a game? What if the same ten women line up two by two from downstage to upstage? Are children walking to school? A choir? What if that same group in the same placement were all facing upstage? Is it more menacing this way? Does facing upstage suggest a different narrative? A different emotion?

In music, ABA describes a bookended theme or ABACADA, a specific refrain that alternates with stanzas or differing themes. This can be applied to dance making where one letter refers to a movement or a phrase, for example. *Accumulation*, using the same example, might be A, AB, ABC, and *rewinding* would be ABC, AB, A. Rewinding can be applied to phrasing, individual steps, or any portion of either of these within a piece. One could choose to *invert* as well as rewind, which would result in CBA, BA, A.

Ordering and reordering by these means or with any methodology the choreographer devises create a familiarity within the progression of a piece of choreography. These examples fall under the umbrella of *sequencing* for which there are limitless possibilities. I have a few choreographer-friends who love math and use these devices and attribute numbers to steps or phrases and then have a ton of fun adding numbers together, which results in new combinations of movement from existing steps.

There are all sorts of devices that add texture, depth, and shading to movement of soloists or groups. *Cut and paste* is just like using Microsoft Word on your computer. You take a phrase or movement or sequence, and using it as is or altering slightly, you add it to another portion of the dance or repeat it within another phrase. Closely aligned with this

CHOREOGRAPHIC FLOWCHART   93

idea is *theme and variation*. If you start with a basic eight-count phrase, for example, one can add nuance through theme and variation by editing or altering part of it, taking the resulting new steps, and adding them to the original phrase. The resulting phrase bears a resemblance to the original but contains some changes that make it unique. There may be an element that refers back to the original statement, but it contains changes, growth, or development in some way. I think all of the Laban tools fall under this subcategory of shading, of changes in energy or force to aid with communication. Playing with effort or space, for example, provides a myriad of options for emphasizing or adding subtlety to your thematic material.

Transposition is simply taking movements or phrases that are already created and applying them to a new part of your body. Legs and arms get used extensively in dance, but have you considered what a rond de jambe might look like if it's performed with your head? Or shoulder? Consider taking a sixteen-count phrase and breaking it up so that it's performed with your right hip and then your left knee. What part of the phrasing is restricted by the natural regulation of the joints? Are there elements that can be carried out more fully? How does the material change shape? Transposition can serve to highlight an important phrase or as a means of theme and variation or cut and paste. It can call attention to something important. This can also be a wonderful tool for getting unstuck when you feel like you're staring at a blank page.

Timing falls within these bounds both in regard to the speed of individual movements and momentum between phrases and individuals on stage. It helps the choreographer to speak. Dances comprised of, for example, ten minutes of repeating eight-count phrases can be repetitive. Pieces with only repeating phrases can lull your audience into a trance state. However, you can use a repeating pattern of music for the benefit of the piece if you eventually want to surprise the viewer. Maybe you paint in white for ten minutes to create an opportunity, to build anticipation toward a slash of red.

Mixing tempos, time signatures, and slicing and dicing when and how you execute steps is exciting. Using a piece of music with a consistent steady tempo needn't be confining. After all, ten counts of eight could also be six counts of nine + a ten count + three counts of two + a five count + a three count + two single counts. It is like making change but with music.

It is a wonderful challenge to divide up music into component parts and force it to say what you want it to say. So there's a huge crescendo on count eight? Don't let it dictate what you do. Could you do your leap on count six and roll to the floor on counts seven and eight? How could that be interpreted? Does it add to your story? If not, try something else. But if it speaks to you, it has the potential to send an electric charge through the audience because they weren't expecting it. Dancing in fours to a waltz? That could be exciting. Are the inflections in the music counter to the movement? What does it say when you swim upstream in this manner? How does it feel if, after five minutes of dancing in fours to a waltz, you all of a sudden give in to the three? Riveting? Freeing? Exciting?

Pathways are a subtle nod to the communicative power of movement. They can play the same role for soloists (although they can be used for groups) that formations serve multiple dancers. Although an audience might not recognize that dance about the Bermuda triangle started upstage left, came down the stage on a diagonal to downstage center, continued on moving on the diagonal to upstage right, and finished where it began, the actual pathway of the dance alludes to the thematic material. Typically, audiences aren't afforded a birds-eye view (although my students have made interesting work with a video camera sitting high in the light grid above the center stage and projecting its image onto the upstage cyclorama). But using spatial patterns as part of your dance making can open up new avenues of thought in spatial design while also contributing thematically to the dance. Pathways can also be used quite effectively in research for movement material.

2. I call the following *tools of external structure* because they are a means of sculpting space. These can be very simple like *mirroring* where two or more dancers' movements are the same but in opposition (as if one dancer were moving in front of a mirror), concepts of dancing *in unison* and *out of unison*, positions in space that are *symmetrical* or *asymmetrical*, contrasts in *levels* and *facings* between and within groups, and where, when, and how individuals or groups of individuals enter and leave the stage, and *transitions* between phrase and sections. They are all part of visually designing space. When I am considering these elements, I look at the *negative space* between bodies as well as the bodies themselves to help me craft the visual sculpture that I seek.

Spatial tools can also comprise any sort of *personal rules* that you create for yourself. As mentioned, when I made *Veil of Ignorance*, I decided I never wanted either dancer in the duet to fully stand up, and I wanted them to share one another's weight for the majority of the piece. I set boundaries and challenged myself to stay within them. Creating your own limits in this way can spur creativity and imagination.

What does it mean when the stage is *balanced*? If these same ten women were split five on either side of center stage in the shape of dots on a die, the stage would be balanced. Take two from the stage left and move them upstage right standing shoulder to shoulder, and the stage becomes unbalanced. Which option is more interesting? I go back to basic art rules here when I note that unbalanced spaces are more eye catching. They draw attention because they aren't in harmony. How does that help or hinder the composer? What does it mean to have four dancers spread evenly across the center stage? How does it change your interpretation when you move two of the dancers downstage right and face them toward one another, one just right of center facing the audience, and the fourth upstage center? How is the dance speaking through this stage setup? How is it different from the original four evenly spaced with a common facing? What can we infer from these placements? How do they forward the theme, the plot, and the story? Or maybe it's just interesting to the eye?

In the same way that balanced stages are restful to the eye so are symmetrical ones. *Symmetrical* stages are comforting, like soup cans lined up on a grocery store shelf or stacked shoe boxes. There is a static association. *Asymmetry* in design is eye catching. In an asymmetrical stage, the space between dancers is challenging. There is tension and vibration. Dealing with asymmetry requires the choreographer to consider balance in a new way. In design, objects that are bigger carry more weight and those that are smaller carry less. If you think of standing downstage in terms of size and weight, the dancer is closer to the audience, which means she is bigger and carries more weight than someone farther away. Therefore, if you put a dancer downstage left, it may take two dancers upstage right to balance her. You may make a choice to only put one dancer upstage right because you want a portion of your dance to be unbalanced. You may want your audience to feel uneasy or uncomfortable.

Balance is a communicative device, but it should be a conscious choice based on the piece you are making, not an accident caused by not thinking it through. Also associated with balance is *formation*. I've seen way too many dances where ten dancers are lined up in two rows of five facing the audience. This obviously is an example where formation isn't helping to communicate (unless you are making a piece about soldiers or maybe a marching band). The formations, the shapes the dancers are making, as well as the negative space between bodies can be a subtle force in communication. What does it mean when four dancers make up a triangle? It is asymmetrical, it is three-sided but contains four people. What if it's situated upstage left? How does that make you feel?

Canon can be structured within time or counts à la "Row, Row, Row Your Boat," where one group begins and after a designated amount of time, or through cues, or even randomly, other groups follow and repeat the movement. In its simplest form, this means that each group ends the phrase with exactly the same number of counts between them. Combining elements like "rewinding-canon" could mean that a previous canon, for example, four groups of two each moving three counts after the next, is performed a second time, but each step is performed backward within the same canon, or each step is performed forward but the canon is reversed. Similarly, you could have an accumulating canon where, after each rotation, a new movement is added. There are limitless possibilities for pairing any of these tools together.

Contrast is a powerful tool. If you are making a mostly abstract piece, for example, once begun, the audience understands and accepts the voice through which you are speaking. If then, for example, six minutes into the dance you choose to stop moving, pause, and smile at the audience—a gesture that is almost universally understood—it is powerful. For six minutes, the audience had been lulled into a sense of understanding, there was an unspoken agreement that abstraction was your language. However, in this instance, the choreographer mixed abstraction with literal movement. Choosing this literal element is tantamount to a needle scratch across the record. It's like an exclamation point. A streak of thick red paint on a light blue canvas.

This is a method to underline a point, to catch audience members off guard, to ensure people are paying attention, and to disrupt their expectations. One must just use tools with thought, with care.

There are many ways to categorize these types of movement tools. Splitting them into two groups is a clear way to differentiate between groups and solo work (internal and external structure). The included second graph also divides the same information in terms of relationship. It looks at movement in relationship to the stage itself, like directions and facings, movement in relationship to the single dancer, which aligns quite closely with the internal structure list, and movement in relationship to other dancers, which aligns closely with the external list. There are many ways to break down movement tools, and there are many other tools not included here. I recommend creating a list of tools and then challenging yourself to continually add new choreographic devices to the list.

E. Integration

This is exactly as it sounds. This is where the puzzle pieces are looked at, rotated, placed, and then cut up, moved around, gathered together, tried, recorded, responded to, reordered, and tried again. It's where we critically evaluate the shading and texturization of the piece and how it relates to the thematic material, how it is shaped and molded, the outgrowth of theatrical elements, and where we first begin to see all of the elements working in harmony. This is where design happens. As you can see, integration flows back into the flowchart at many points and then flows back down in more trials. This circular motion and feeding of ideas back into inspiration, research, theme, and development become a waterwheel that converts ideas into dance.

As integration progresses, I leave you with two points to consider:

1. As mentioned earlier, I caution my students that if they can give a name to a step, to consider doing something different. When working toward authentic movement, why perform a grand battement when you can lift the leg in a different way that has not been named? Maybe flex the foot and bend the knee as the leg is lifted, bring the

leg to shoulder height, then point the toe and bend your supporting leg? That movement doesn't have a name.

This *naming* game serves as a tool to encourage young choreographers to break out of a predefined vocabulary. It encourages the exploration of new movement ideas. It causes them to stop and give thought to what a movement is actually saying rather than just stringing a series of dance movements together. The hope is that it will create interesting movements, movements we've never seen before, and movements that can communicate what the maker intends. Young choreographers, quite understandably, use what they are taught. Typically, they have been taking dance classes for ten or fifteen years by the time they get to college. They've had hundreds of hours of technique and have learned which steps go with other steps. My students who have studied classical ballet haven't encountered a tombé that doesn't have a pas de bourrée following it. Therefore, whenever they choreograph a tombé, we know what's coming next. Audiences are the same. One chaîné usually becomes two or three because they're taught in succession.

What do five turns say that one turn can't? Maybe nothing. Maybe something. Sometimes repetitive movement or phrasing is thematically necessary. It's an engaging choreographic practice, though, to keep the audience guessing. It's so exciting when a tombé turns into something else, when a glissade turns into a floor roll, when a run doesn't end in a leap. It's the same idea as the option to not dance in eights to music set in eights. A useful tool for a choreographer is to run counter to what is expected. *Disruption* is a marvelous tool.

2. Keeping audiences guessing, disrupting their expectations is just a shorthand way of expressing the goal of using choreographic tools in unique and exciting ways. I spend more time than I'd like asking some version of this question of my students, "What is your tombé, pas de bourrée, glissade, grand jeté *saying*?"

A list of ballet vocabulary strung together doesn't necessarily *say* anything. But if you stop and break apart the pieces, shade part of it, underline others, switch up directions, and reverse a few elements, what happens? If you face upstage for part of it and perform the last

CHOREOGRAPHIC FLOWCHART 99

bit in double time, is it beginning to speak? In what way? What are the tools you can use to make your movement talk to the audience, express an emotion, or tell a story? Using colors and shading, texturizing, and smearing creates an interesting palate and by choosing your tools wisely, with care and dexterity, can help you tell your story. Each step must be a conscious decision born out of thought, experimentation, and communicative intent. It's important to remember that each choice must serve the artistic intent and thematic material.

Tools Guide

INTERNAL STRUCTURE	EXTERNAL STRUCTURE
Accumulation	Mirroring
Rewind	Canon
Transposition	Symmetry/Asymmetry
Cut & paste	Formations
Levels	Synchronous/Asynchronous
Timing	Transitions
Facings	Balance
Placement	Rules
Pathways	Space/Negative space
Sequencing	Contrasting/Same
Theme & variation	
Invert	
Reverse	
Laban tools	

Dancer in relationship with stage	Dancer in relationship with self	Dancer in relationship with other dancers
Facings	Accumulation	Mirroring
Placement	Rewind	Synchronous/Asynchronous
Balance	Invert	Symmetrical/Asymmetrical
Pathways	Transitions	Canon
Space	Levels	Contrasting/Same
Formations	Transposition	
Shape	Cut & Paste	
	Theme & Variation	
	Timing	
	Laban tools	
	Sequencing	
	Reverse	

Figure 5.5 Tools guide.
Credit: ©Jenefer Davies, 2022.

III. Production

The following production elements are in no particular order. I put them after the main body of the flowchart not because they aren't important. They are important. I separate them from practice because these elements are often a collaboration between the choreographer and the designer. Ideas relating to production elements, however, should be integral to the choreographer's process.

Choreographic ideas can be expanded upon by considering, for example, the place of sets, lighting, or video projection in your dance. These elements should be a living organism that contributes to, reflect, and change as the flowchart work is happening. In this way, as the piece develops, these elements communicate with the other facets of the work and begin to take shape. I can't tell you the number of times that I've seen my students work for months and months on a piece and, at the last minute, add a theatrical element they'd been planning the entire time but never physically incorporated. For example, there was a dance that involved a thirty-foot-long piece of fabric. Because they'd been working with rehearsal fabric and the actual fabric wasn't introduced until tech week, the dancers realized too late that the fabric was too heavy to throw into the air. Or a piece required chairs of a certain height and weight, but the rehearsal chairs were lighter than the performance chairs. When the time came to move into the theater and use the performance chairs, the dancers couldn't lift them with the speed necessary for the choreography. Or finally, a piece with fog was never experimented with ahead of time so the dancers didn't realize until too late that our fog machine couldn't be finely tuned and generated very thick fog. They realized they wouldn't be able to see one another for cueing. These practical problems, had they been worked out sooner, could have been more easily solved. The choreographic ramifications are much larger. Had these considerations been incorporated into the pieces as they were being made, the resulting performance piece may have been much different. The play between the set piece or the fog element and the movement may have inspired new movement ideas. Some small changes in chair weight might have caused ripples through the flowchart and affected the phrasing, the costuming, or other elements. It's the butterfly effect but with dance.

Moreover, these sorts of elements are generally in the piece for symbolic or representational purposes, so changing them can disrupt the overall theme of the piece. They can't be an afterthought. They have to be integrated from the start. Working with designers from the initial first sparks of inspiration routinely leads to interesting, unintended, creative breakthroughs and new movement ideas. Working with theatrical elements from the beginning of the process can also aid in clarifying empty or confusing places by focusing your attention and giving yourself the time to work them into the overall composition.

An example of the way in which incorporating production elements into the choreographic process (and communicating with the designers throughout) can aid a work-in-progress lies with a piece I made over twenty years ago. This dance dealt with the versatility and stamina it takes to be a woman. It was a lighthearted piece that explored the irony in women bearing both the extreme pain of childbirth and being called "the weaker sex." In one section, I experimented with dance movements that gave the impression of something heavy being tossed, but I didn't like how it looked. I couldn't put my finger on the problem. Later, when working on another section that dealt with other matters, I wanted to create a moment of levity by turning the dancers upstage, and when they turned back to the audience, they'd have fake pregnant bellies. When discussing these ideas with my designer, he said simply, "A basketball would solve both problems." That phrase shifted my thinking. In the end, not only did that contribution give me the freedom to move forward in a new way but the inspiration and the information garnered from walking down an unexplored path fueled the creation of the rest of the dance.

I find myself having to remind my students repeatedly that a designer is not someone whose job it is to do whatever the choreographer asks. A designer is an artist and a partner. A choreographer must have good communication skills to be able to articulate their vision, their thematic material, their plans, and goals to the designer. The designer then absorbs the information, translates it into their art form, and comes back with ideas. From there, discussion and debate shape the overall piece. Because so much of working with collaborators (and budgets!) is compromise, choreographers must be open and flexible with their plans. This flexibility means they must create alternative options should their ideas be too expensive, too difficult to build/create, conflicting with commitments the shop has to other productions, or not possible for some other reason.

Healthy communication and compromise are essential, and I've found that many times working through practical issues like cost or theater space or time limitations can lead to greater creativity and solutions that end up better than the original idea. Sometimes this process can be daunting for new choreographers as they feel that they barely know what their dance is when they have to explain it to someone else. However, verbalizing the thematic material and discussing it with another person brings awareness to areas that might be weak or not fully thought through. Hearing another's interpretation of your work, after being so close to it for so long, can be a refreshing reset and a new perspective worth considering. (This is also why it's a great idea to talk about your work with colleagues and friends. Sometimes being too close to your work can be artistically stifling.) It's also one of many reasons that I regularly use Liz Lerman's Critical Response Process in my classes.[11] It's a wonderful tool to help teach young choreographers how to speak about dance.

Figure 5.6 Cruel beauty.
Credit: ©Washington and Lee University 2008.

Lerman's process involves four steps that ground the work in discussion of the movement while also protecting the creator by putting the power in their hands. After seeing the work, the audience responds with what was meaningful, challenging, provocative, etc. to them in what they saw. The artist asks questions of the responders that they can answer, and then the responders have a chance to ask neutral questions devoid of opinion. Although students occupy a vulnerable position in front of their peers, I love this process because it protects the creator. Responders may only give opinions if invited by the artist. The entire process is guided by a leader or a teacher to keep people on task and obeying the guidelines. This experience trains young choreographers and dancers to think clearly about what they want to say and the way in which they say it before speaking. Valuable tools.

Figure 5.7 Cruel beauty.
Credit: ©Washington and Lee University 2008.

A. Costumes

How can your thematic material be expressed through costumes? What material, pattern, color is reflective of what you want to say? How can it shape or frame your intent? How does the fabric play with your movement? While some fabrics may look amazing and fit your exact vision, if they can't stretch or move in the way that is necessary for the dance, they won't do service to your work. Most dances require a costume to behave in a certain way. The piece based on the movement of the ocean, for example, will probably need to flow with a lightness that enables the material to float in the air before falling. It's unusual in my experience for a tight, bound costume to be desired, but I made a solo once, Cruel Beauty, that dealt with feeling trapped. I discussed my thematic material with a costume designer, and she devised a red and black halter top for me whose neckties extended down and wrapped around my neck, ribs, and waist. I put it on and felt like my torso was in a straitjacket. It appeared as if someone had tied me up, but the ties seemed to grow out and around me from an internal place underneath the costume. To me, the garment's binding produced an effect in me reminiscent of a panic attack. My breathing was constricted, my ribs were constrained. She physically depicted my story through her design. Interestingly, when I wore it to rehearse, the constriction informed the movement. I made edits to my choreography that were not only necessary due to the physicality of the costume, but they served also to illustrate this real restriction. Designs aren't always as concrete as this, obviously, and can involve abstraction through color, shape, or flow of material, among other things. Cruel Beauty example stands out in my mind because the costume had a literal effect on the dance.

VIDEO REFERENCE 5.1

Cruel Beauty

Re-watching this piece makes me cringe. I include it here because it's a clear example of a healthy costumer/choreographer relationship with clear, thematic material reflected in the design. However, I considered deeply whether to leave it out. I hesitated because I don't want to share something that carries with it an insensitivity to race. But I realized that this is a good example for young makers of what not to do. I cringe not because of the choreography although this piece does need quite a bit of work to bring it into the realm of artistic comfort for me.

The unforgivable error I made was not choosing the music in a thoughtful way. "A Change Is Gonna Come," written by Sam Cooke and sung by Otis Redding, is a soulful, spiritual anthem for the Civil Rights Era. It addresses racism and channels Cooke's own personal experiences as a representative of the Black experience in America.

I'm bringing attention to this because it's a shining example of a poor, uninformed artistic choice. It's the epitome of white centering and the ignorant appropriation of another race's experience. I chose it because it spoke to me, but I neglected to recognize that this is not my story to tell. My story isn't comparable in any way, shape, or form to the narrative in this music. In my privileged whiteness, I took it and I used it as my own. I'm ashamed and embarrassed that I made this choice. I never performed the piece again nor do I ever intend to. I only include it here as a caution. Think as you make choices. Be aware and inclusive of those around you. Do your research. Work to de-center your view. I will write more about music later but this particular piece of choreography and the uninformed choice I made had to be addressed.

Figure 5.8 Aerial dance.
Credit: ©Washington and Lee University 2008.

A piece that I made in 2009 is an example of how costumes can augment what is already happening in a dance. The initial aerial dance performance that I created for Washington and Lee University was an exercise in firsts. We were one of the first colleges in the country to teach aerial, and to my knowledge, I was the first person to create an academic program in aerial dance. This was the first dance of the first concert in the first year of the aerial program.

My goal when making this work was to give my students an experiential outcome to augment their classroom work. They were new aerial dancers, and I had never worked with this particular aerial rigging company. We'd never performed outside on the wall of our building, so I wanted to give them material that was challenging enough for them as dancers but didn't push them so hard that they felt unsuccessful. So I made a fairly simple dance and used a piece of music with a steady, simple rhythm.

Our costume designer, Jessica Miller, used the simplicity of the dance as a counterpoint to the complexity of the costume. She created three fluffy, colorful confections with multiple layers of lightweight fabric primed for moving through the air. They each had colorful forty-foot trains that accentuated their height. While the dance itself didn't push boundaries movement-wise (apart from its aerial nature), the costumes had lives of their own. They pulsed and flowed and traced the paths of the dancers. They spun when the dancers spun, and there were occasions when the trains were held aloft, frozen in space for a few moments. They were like floating veils. They appeared to be lighter than air. They were breath made visible. She may not have designed these costumes in this way if she hadn't been present in rehearsals, watched rehearsal videos, and discussed the piece with me. While not many choreographers may desire for their costumes to play such a prominent role, for me, this was the perfect marriage of daring dancers and flying fabrics.

VIDEO REFERENCE 5.2

Aerial Dance

I've always wanted to make a dance whose costumes are completely made out of paper and staples. I'd like to create the dance based on the sounds the paper makes during movement and the ways in which movement and the dancer's moving body can change the shape and texture of the costume. I can imagine experimentation with different weights and thicknesses of paper and decisions might be based on what was visually and auditorily appealing.

Of course, a new paper costume would have to be made for every experimentation session, every rehearsal, and each performance. This immediately brings to mind concerns regarding budget, time, and resources. But by virtue of the project's strengths and limitations, it would require a close collaboration between choreographer, designer, and dancer. Such a collaboration is immensely exciting, where all artists are equally tasked with daily refinements to their contribution, and their interaction is fluid and experimental from one day to the next. It would be wonderful if one day all dances could be made collaboratively.

One of the most important responsibilities of the choreographer is keeping the costume designer in the loop. In most cases, the piece is being created from a concept, and because of this, composition will be fluid. Ideas will grow, and through trial and error, changes will be made. It's important to stay in communication with your designer, invite her/him/them to rehearsals, and upload and send videos. Stay in touch.

B. Set

How can set pieces, set decoration, or props augment and help tell your story? Do you need pieces to fly in or out? Will you be using battens? Do you need pieces built for your dance and, if so, do they need to carry the weight of the dancers? If they are on the set, will the dancers be still or in motion? These sorts of questions help determine how set pieces will be constructed.

Dancers in motion carry force, torque, imbalances, and weight shifts. Dancers can affect how set pieces move and the integrity of the set piece itself. These details are important and if not communicated properly can affect the successful performance of the dance and the safety of the dancers.

108 CHOREOGRAPHIC FLOWCHART

Figure 5.9 M(other).
Credit: ©Washington and Lee University 2016.

Dancing on the rolling circular platform in m(other), for example, took quite a lot of rehearsal. A portion of the rehearsal was simply becoming acclimated to the size and shape of the piece, but I also wanted dancers moving on the platform both in tandem with the way it was being turned and in opposition to it. I wanted stillness and held lifts on the platform as well as transitions and phrases. Because the platform was resting on wheels, it was a constant challenge to

Figure 5.10 M(other).
Credit: ©Washington and Lee University 2016.

balance on it, and of course, I wanted the dancers on the platform to look as if they were unaffected by these transitions. Additionally, because the platform was moved and manipulated by people, there was potential for human error both from those dancing on the set piece and from those moving the set piece.

Although I linked to this piece earlier in the book, I will include the link here again, so you don't have to flip backward to find it. This rolling cart was choreographed into this piece not just for the dancing sections but also to fix where, at what speed, and how it entered and left the stage. This happened multiple times throughout the piece, and it can be interesting to watch the piece solely for that movement.

VIDEO REFERENCE 5.3

M(other)

The more detailed you can be about the role the set piece plays in your thematic material and the ways in which you imagine working with or using the set or set pieces, the more information the designer has and can work from. It's been my experience that designers have wonderful ideas that can inform the choreographic plan in new, wonderful ways. However, most choreography is born from an idea, and that idea grows and morphs over time through rehearsals, which designers generally are not present for.

So it's important that as things develop and challenges arise, you keep the lines of communication open with your set designer. I video all my students' pieces weekly and upload it to a site that my set designer has access to. This is a great way to keep him/her/them informed but has to be followed up with explanations and conversations. Weekly meetings to discuss these updates are a great idea.

Another example of the use of props in dance is *Breathing Lessons*. I made this piece to question the link between our ability to breathe and a physical clue to our spiritual or psychological condition. If we are so stressed that taking a deep breath is difficult or if we are panicked by events that make breathing labored, our bodies react of their own accord. Conversely, when something takes our breath away or something beautiful leaves us breathless, it is a gentle, sweeter breath but one that's equally unpredictable.

CHOREOGRAPHIC FLOWCHART 111

Figure 5.11 Breathing Lessons.
Credit: ©Washington and Lee University 2014.

Figure 5.12 Breathing Lessons.
Credit: ©Washington and Lee University 2014.

This dance is an exploration of the many facets of breath, its interpretation, and the discoveries we can make about ourselves. I used fans as props to mimic breath in a person but also to represent an external force exerted upon the body. In this dance, the wind is a constant force that the dancer fights. It molds her and causes her to move in a labored way, pushes her down, and causes the struggle. I sought to physicalize that force and the ramifications of it. At the start of the piece, the dancer is wrapped and harnessed to fabric, something that can be beautiful when it's set free but is restrictive and binding in this scenario. Along with the conflict is the veiled suggestion that what looks like weakness isn't. It's because of her strength that she's able to fight.

VIDEO REFERENCE 5.4

Breathing Lessons

I made a piece in 2019 that, based on all the other work I've made, could be described as a palate cleanser. At the time I made it, I'd been making serious work for a few years, and I decided to revive an old piece from many years earlier that was a bit lighter.

Blame Game is a look at love and loss from vantage points of both strength and sorrow. My signature deep rooted, grounded movement with thematic undercurrents of female empowerment are present, but the dance doesn't take itself too seriously. Frenzied and a bit bipolar movement-wise, it was choreographed to speak to the low points in human lives yet encourages us to look on the bright side with humor and a bit of fun.

The overly dramatic story is punctuated with oversized boxing gloves, a huge spool containing a ream of paper, numerous tissue boxes, and very specific choreographic moments with the boxes and individual tissues. While not seen, the effects of a specially constructed platform and lever mounted high above the lighting grid on center stage made their debut in the last few seconds of the dance. Our technical director built this contraption using the set designer's

Figure 5.13 Blame Game.
Credit: ©Washington and Lee University 2019.

schematics, which were defined and discussed between the two of us as I was creating the work.

The props manager and costume designer together worked to find appropriately sized boxing gloves, fitting the gloves to the dancer with special attachments so they can be put on and taken off quickly, and yet were light enough to be danced in. They fit well with the thematic and practical needs of the dance, and the fact that they were bright red was a bonus. The tossing, sliding, and exchanging of boxes is highly choreographed and required balance and coordination. Fine motor skills were evident when dancers pulled tissues out of the boxes with their toes.

We had a few discussions during the creation of this piece concerning what constitutes a prop and if a costume piece that doesn't serve a typical costume purpose could be considered a prop. General thinking is that if you carry something, it's considered a prop but if you wear it, it's a costume. For the purposes of this dance, we considered the boxing gloves props because although they were worn some of the time, they spent more time being manipulated, thrown around, and caught. During a semester of rehearsals, we went through boxes and boxes of tissues, which the prop manager bought in bulk.

VIDEO REFERENCE 5.5

Blame Game

C. Lighting

How can lighting help you tell your story? Express your emotion? Support your theme? Does your piece feel warm or cold? Bright or dim? Do you picture the stage fully lit or partially lit? Do you see spotlights in your dance? Area lights? Gobos? Many times, lighting designers working with first-time choreographers will ask these questions as a starting point. Broad questions like this give the lighting designer clues as to your plans.

Many times, first production meetings are early on in the creative process so specific thematic material hasn't been set yet or isn't ready

CHOREOGRAPHIC FLOWCHART 115

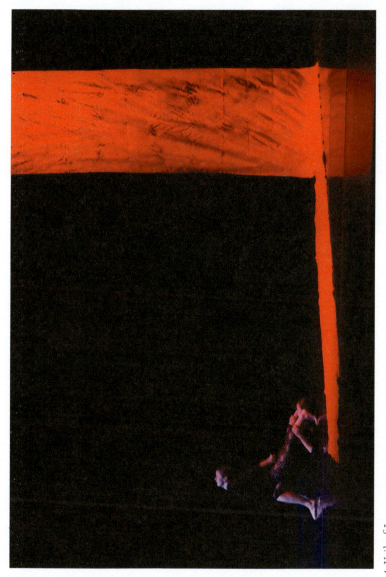

Figure 5.14 Veil of Ignorance.
Credit: ©Washington and Lee University 2016.

Figure 5.15 Veil of Ignorance.
Credit: ©Washington and Lee University 2016.

to be viewed. These early meetings provide opportunities to begin a conversation. As was the case when discussing sets and costumes, having excellent communication skills will aid your lighting designer in his/her/their work. If you can clearly explain your overarching theme, what you're trying to say and how you plan to communicate it, it will give them a starting point. Then, later, when you've got material to share, you can expound upon the earlier conversations and begin to include specific material and goals.

A choreographic piece with beautiful lighting design by my colleague, Shawn Paul Evans, is *Veil of Ignorance*. He was skillful in a subtle yet powerful design. This is a very quiet, very still duet that could easily be overpowered by too much lighting. The duet is a comment on being, at once, both detached and interdependent, alone yet with someone else. It is a glimpse into a broken, toxic relationship.

The dance was created with the intent that no dancer would ever stand completely upright. They lean, support, and hold one another in an interdependent way. I played with combining their two bodies into one such that it appears at times, for example, as though they have one torso but four legs or two connected heads with one body. At the start of the piece, Evans deftly lit only the dancers' feet, keeping their bodies in the darkness, which created the illusion of walking on water or air. He slowly incorporated gobos as the bodies began to move but lit only exactly the space that was necessary, leaving the rest in darkness. He made subtle and carefully edited choices at the start of the piece and later used lighting to enhance the choreography and intensify the dramatic narrative. A long canvas drape, hung from a batten high above the stage, was a central figure in the piece, yet dancers never interacted with it. The way the fabric was hung traced a path through the imagined sky onto the floor. Although it was static, the lighting designer made it look like it was on fire, calmly burning while the dance ensued. This red scenic piece leads the way out, but no one takes the path.

VIDEO REFERENCE 5.6

Veil of Ignorance

Another example of a deftly lit piece, ... in these cases, a few seconds of pause, was grounded in the dynamics and interactions of discussion and the ways in which we listen, process, and respond. It is a window into personality, individuality, and community with attention to the power of persuasion and the loneliness/power dynamic of independent thinking. It is the embodiment of social interaction and a comment on what it means to be an introvert who is brimming with ideas but can't express them.

This nebulous concept called for an inventive hand and the ability to use lighting to underscore the fluctuation of the spoken word along with a heightened sense of volume and tempo within speech patterns. For this reason, I worked closely again with my colleague and fellow artist, Shawn Paul Evans. The lighting played the essential role of not just defining but also enabling the thematic material.

118   CHOREOGRAPHIC FLOWCHART

Figure 5.16 ... in these cases, a few seconds of pause.
Credit: ©Washington and Lee University 2018.

By lighting a downstage narrowly defined corridor, he created a "talking" space. Dancers moved forward into the light alone, in pairs, or at overlapping intervals to define the conversation through movement. Dancers in darkness were silent. As the piece grows, the conversation slowly becomes more chaotic until the lights are forced to open up creating a larger space that encompasses bigger movement that can travel through space. From a thematic viewpoint, this looks like argument, debate, heightened emotions. The codependency of lighting and movement made this piece a wonderful opportunity for partnership. The collaboration between Evans and myself had to begin early and had to continue weekly because the piece grew slowly, and we both were shaping it in real time.

It would be so easy to overwhelm a dance like this with production elements. The piece is partially in silence and almost meditative in its patterns. Evans used lighting to bring focus to specific elements of the conversation but never disrupted or interrupted the dialogue.

VIDEO REFERENCE 5.7

... in these cases, a few seconds of pause

An earlier incarnation of this idea was a 2016 piece called *The Conversation*. It was a quartet that was simply one ten-minute piece that explored layering conversation onto bodies. You can see most of the choreography translated to the later work in some format.

Clearly the piece was later refined, a solo was added to the beginning, and the music, sound, and silence score were completely overhauled. Apart from this, what's interesting when looking back at the original performance is the stark contrast in lighting. The video from 2016 was for a performance at the Center for Performance Research in Brooklyn for which I didn't have a designer. You can see the beginnings of the idea of stepping into and out of light to recognize speech, but clearly, it wasn't refined.

It never ceases to amaze me what a beautiful symbiotic relationship exists between choreographers and lighting designers. A dance can be transformed, brought to its fullest potential, or, sadly, the opposite, depending on your designer's artistic skills, your communicative powers, and your working relationship. (You may remember from an earlier chapter when I discussed my work m(other)? If this dance seems similar, it's because it is. I loved the second section of that dance that I took the

Figure 5.17 The Conversation.
Credit: Courtesy of Taylor Jones, 2018.

basic idea and explored, played with it, and expanded upon it. It became *The Conversation* and then it later became ... *in these cases, a few seconds of pause.* Tracing the lineage of choreography is fascinating.)

VIDEO REFERENCE 5.8

The Conversation

Lighting is so intrinsically tied to dance that I will add a third example to show another choreographer/designer relationship. *August & September* is, in effect, two duets performed in sequence and again simultaneously. The piece plays with time suggesting the same relationship at two different moments. The interaction consists of weight sharing, catches, and holds. There is a closeness, an intimacy between the partners in the pairs. The synergy is similar but more sophisticated in the mature relationship.

The two couples watch one another across the chasm but that is their only interaction. This piece was frustrating to create because while they were connected thematically, it was difficult to relate their connection visually. My lighting designer, again Shawn Paul Evans (who is so

Figure 5.18 August & September.
Courtesy of Emma Davies-Mansfield, 2016.

talented), managed to isolate both pairs using lighting, so it appeared as though their bodies glowed from inside the darkness that surrounded them, yet he connected them with soft glows when they were in stillness and a gentle rise in intensity when they began to move. Again, it was a lovely, skillful design because it allowed you to see only the pairs, and it defined their importance at varying times with levels. One was never more important than the other, but the lighting focused in on each pair when necessary. The effect was to alternately cast one and then the other pair in an otherworldly aura to communicate the idea they were watching each other from different points in time.

VIDEO REFERENCE 5.9

August & September

D. Media

I use "media" as an overarching term that encompasses video, photography, social media, or any digital form used in the dance, front or rear projection, essentially any visual element that is not dance, costumes, sets, or lighting. My students use media more frequently now than in the past five years or so. I think because college-aged students are so well versed in technology when they arrive on campus, they seek to incorporate it into their art making.

The addition of media to a piece of dance has the potential to introduce very exciting elements, as the media provides more nuanced layers to the overall artwork. Like all of these production elements, they need to be designed, organized, incorporated and explored as the dance is being made. Too often I've seen dances that have been completed before consideration is given to video or projection. It's important for young choreographers to create their dances holistically. As they are devising movement phrases, they should be thinking about digital or other elements.

The movement and media should inform and inspire one another. In this way, the piece grows organically and, should something not work, it can be edited and either replaced or left out as the piece is created. These elements inform and play off of the dance and vice versa. The relationship between movement and media is important to respect.

122 CHOREOGRAPHIC FLOWCHART

Figure 5.19 La Fentêre.
Credit: ©Washington and Lee University 2017.

CHOREOGRAPHIC FLOWCHART 123

Figure 5.20 La Fentêre.
Credit: ©Washington and Lee University 2017.

Figure 5.21 La Fentêre.
Credit: ©Washington and Lee University 2017.

A good example of media being integrated into a choreographic work is a piece I made a few years ago called *La Fenêtre*. The larger theme of the piece dealt with 1940s café culture as a center of political, social, and cultural life. It explores the dynamics of conversation and debate and the blurring of the distinctions of class and social status. To help tell this story, I decided to look at the human body as it is and in relationship to photography projections.

I projected photos of café culture—people sitting at outdoor cafes in 1940s Paris. The images were projected onto a forty by sixty feet cyclorama upstage. A curtain then lowered, and when the curtain rose again, the photograph was still there but the images of people were replaced with student dancers in exactly the same place, wearing the same clothes, and doing the same things as the original image. I played with perspective so that the dancers fit into the image as three-dimensional objects on a two-dimensional graphic. I loved that it tricked the eye, and the physicality of replacing images with people was exciting. The concept of an image literally jumping off of a page grounded the audience in the 1940s and gave me the opportunity to tell my story visually as well as kinesthetically.

VIDEO REFERENCE 5.10

La Fenêtre

Another, although wholly different, example of media in dance is a collaboration I did in 2011 with my brother, who is an economics professor at Duquesne University. Antony is a researcher in experimental economics, and we thought it would be interesting to use dance to exhibit an economic principle. We chose the *Tragedy of the Commons* because we felt that the subject matter was manageable and because it deals with resources, we felt we could make a connection to performance.

During the show, five volunteers sat at a bank of computers from which they were able to control five spotlights, each with the capability to illuminate one dancer. The volunteers were instructed to keep their dancers lit as much as possible. During the first part of the dance, the volunteers shared a bank of time, and once that time was exhausted, the dancers were in darkness. If, however, they took brief moments with the light off, the bank would replenish itself.

CHOREOGRAPHIC FLOWCHART

Figure 5.22 The Tragedy of the Commons.
Credit: ©Washington and Lee University 2011.

We performed the dance. The volunteers generated a total of five minutes and forty-five seconds of light. Antony then spoke to the audience again. For the second part of the dance, he explained, everything was the same in that the volunteers used light as usual but this time, they used and restored it from private banks of time. During the second movement, when light banks were personally owned, they generated six minutes and forty-four seconds of light. The hypothesis, which the dance supported, is that if people know that they own something, they will take more care of their resources than if it's communally owned because ownership provides them an incentive to conserve.

VIDEO REFERENCE 5.11

The Tragedy of the Commons

This dance was a challenge to make because my goal as choreographer was to provide movement so interesting that someone won't want to turn the light off. It was my goal to challenge the volunteers to have to

126 CHOREOGRAPHIC FLOWCHART

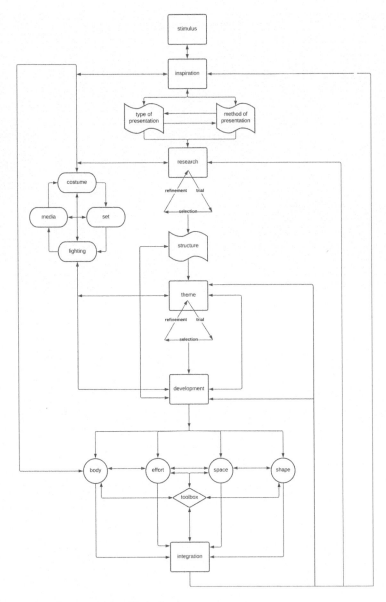

Figure 5.23 Choreographic Flowchart.
Credit: ©Jenefer Davies, 2022.
* Items listed in circles are part of Laban/Bartenieff Fundamentals, "About LIMS®," Laban/Bartenieff Institute of Movement Studies, accessed September 4, 2022, https://labaninstitute.org/about
** Items listed in flags are inspired by Smith-Autard's *Dance Composition: A Practical Guide to Creative Success in Dance Making*, 2004

choose if and when they, in essence, shut off the dance. Choreographing inside a spotlight led to creative space and shape making because the boundary was so defined and area was quite small.

Because the volunteers (and the audience) were watching one dancer in each spotlight and not a concert work, it meant I had to make five solos, each of which had to be compelling and interesting. There was much technology embedded in this project, and it was refreshing for dance to play a role, not the role, in the piece. Other factors were as important as the movement, which made collaboration with my brother and the lighting designer a ton of fun.

IV. An alternative flowchart

A. Flowchart, v2

As mentioned above, I recreated a flowchart that spoke to me and incorporated the way in which I work. I like this adaptation because it both theoretically and physically represents the circular nature of the composition process. Most of the time when I am making a piece, I think I am starting in one place, but I encounter diversions, new ideas, breakthroughs, roadblocks, and culs de sac along the way that shoot me off in new directions. Many times, the very thing that inspired me in the first place ends up being replaced with something more intriguing, challenging, or interesting, and sometimes, after months and months of dedication, I find myself back at the start of the path. This is the frustrating madness of the process, which tests your patience and humility, and belief in yourself yet, inevitably, ends up ... eventually ... with patience ... and work ... in a magical place.

While revising the flowchart, I changed some of the language to suit myself. The first version spoke to those who've had grammar classes, understand the principles of writing, and appreciate an organized path, but this version speaks to the artist, and although it seems quite organized to me, I can understand if the wild nature of its architecture might cause some unease. You may notice also that the meat of the process—the play/improv/decision-making about what movements to include—have been moved up the flowchart into the belly of the image as opposed to the bottom of the image in the first version. This is because when I work, everything that I do grows from my thematic material.

I'm not able to flow through the first five steps or so until I have a grasp on my theme, and, once understood, I move up and down and around the flowchart. From there, each element will influence and alter all the other elements as I move through the chart. In other words, if I had an orange crayon and I traced my path as I made a piece of choreography, there would be a dot on a *theme* where I begin and, from there, it would look like a tangled mess of crosshatching, circles, arrows, gashes moving backward, and furrows moving forwards, up, and down, slashing and scraping, until all the little flowchart boxes were obscured with thick and thin, hard and soft lines of orange. So that you can compare the two charts, below is a little vocabulary key. Apart from these words, the rest are the same. They are just in new positions on the chart. See page 129 for flowchart version 2.

Flowchart		Flowchart v2
integration	=	embodiment
theme	=	silhouette
development	=	design

B. If these flowcharts crush your soul ...

You may not like this flowchart. It may feel stifling or ridged or pedestrian. It may feel as though it kills the creative spark. That's understandable. There are many ways to make dances. Some choreographers use improvisation only and record themselves moving through space with video and then pick the parts they like and set them on dancers. Others come to rehearsal with no pre-set ideas and simply move the dancers around and, many times, use the work that the dancers produce as choreography, moving or adjusting things they see or ideas they like (a practice that should always credit the dancers as choreographers).

What this flowchart does is keep your thematic material and how it relates to moving through space at the forefront of the process. *Steps* aren't all there is to dance. How we move, why we move, and with what

CHOREOGRAPHIC FLOWCHART 129

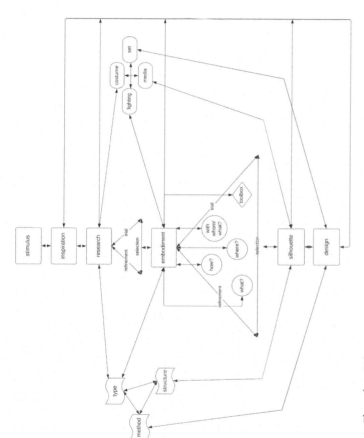

Figure 5.24 Choreographic Flowchart V2.
Credit: ©Jenefer Davies, 2022.

* Items listed in circles are part of Laban/Bartenieff Fundamentals, "About LIMS®," Laban/Bartenieff Institute of Movement Studies, accessed September 4, 2022, https://labaninstitute.org/about

** Items listed in flags are inspired by Smith-Autard's *Dance Composition: A Practical Guide to Creative Success in Dance Making*, 2004

weight, dynamics, and speed all should be answered through the work not as a by-product of *steps*. The questions should be the motivating factor for choosing the movement.

For new choreographers, this flowchart may help them stay on a path and not be distracted by flashy or virtuosic movements that might be beautiful in and of itself but lend nothing to the thematic material of a particular piece. Television shows like *So You Think You Can Dance* and *World of Dance* have stoked and perpetuated choreographers' and audiences' desire for virtuosity and tricks, and while that can be fun, it isn't necessarily indicative of good choreography. I ask my students, what do eight pirouettes say that one cannot?

Further (and this will be discussed later and, in more detail), music is a crafty partner and can, without us knowing it, lead the choreographer astray. In my opinion, music has the same allure for choreographers as it does for children in the Pied Piper story. We willingly follow if the beat of the music speaks to us. This flowchart will help you focus on the movement. Having said all of this, however, don't ever let anyone tell you there is only one way to make a dance.

There is no one right answer. There are a myriad of options. Always feel free to explore, try on various alternatives and see what fits. See what sings to you. Discover what combinations of methodology work for you. Maybe you video yourself improvising, then you upload the footage to iMovie, cut it apart, paste it back together in a new way, and set that material on students? Maybe you painstakingly read, interview people, take notes, and find that when you are present in the studio, your research speaks to you through movement?

I sit in a chair with a pencil and paper. I write down what I see in my head. Sometimes I draw what I see. No studio. No music. All visualization. It helps me to stay focused and not be led astray by music, architecture of the space, or the many phone calls and students that invariably interrupt the process. It's a time for me to download all the many ideas, insights, images, and words that have presented themselves, inspired me, preyed on my mind. I feel sometimes that it's an information dump. I get it on paper so I can see it, and then I reorder it, mold it, throw away parts, and highlight others. By giving it form, I see connections between things. The process always brings up other questions and gives me inspiration so that as I go through the ensuing days or week, I can gather more information and store it for the next visualization session.

I didn't realize I worked like this until trying and failing to work in other ways. It's important to find your path. But, as a means to, or until you do so, it's helpful to have a stencil, tracing paper, a mechanism to help you find your way. This is how the flowchart can be used, as training wheels until you devise or discover your own system.

Notes

1 "About LIMS®," Laban/Bartenieff Institute of Movement Studies, accessed September 4, 2022, https://labaninstitute.org/about

2 Jacqueline Smith-Autard, *Dance Composition: A Practical Guide to Creative Success in Dance Making*, 5th ed. (London: A&C Black Publishers, 2004).

3 Smith-Autard, *Dance Composition*; Lorenzo Pereira, "What is Abstract Art? Meaning and Definition of Art Informel," Widewalls, November 17, 2015, https://www.widewalls.ch/magazine/what-is-abstract-art-informel

4 Smith-Autard, *Dance Composition*; Pereira, "What is Abstract Art?"; "Examples of Symbolism in Art," Literary Devices, accessed September 4, 2022, https://literarydevices.net/examples-of-symbolism-in-art

5 Smith-Autard, *Dance Composition*.

6 "Rudolph Laban," Laban/Bartenieff Institute of Movement Studies, accessed September 4, 2022, https://labaninstitute.org/about/rudolf-laban

7 "Irmgard Bartenieff," Laban/Bartenieff Institute of Movement Studies, accessed September 4, 2022, https://labaninstitute.org/about/irmgard-bartenieff

8 Antja Kennedy, "Laban/Bartenieff Movement Studies for Dance Professionals," *Nordic Journal of Dance* 7,2 (2016): 54–59, https://doi.org/10.2478/njd-2016-0016

9 Vanessa Ewan and Kate Sagovsky, *Laban's Efforts in Action* (London: Bloomsbury Press, 2018).

10 Robin Konie, "A Brief Overview of Laban Movement Analysis", accessed December 28, 2022, http://psychomotorischetherapie.info/website/wp-content/uploads/2015/10/LMA-Workshop-Sheet-Laban.pdf

11 "Critical Response Process," Liz Lerman (website), accessed September 4, 2022, https://lizlerman.com/critical-response-process

6

(THE SEDUCTIVE CUNNING OF) MUSIC

Figure 6.1 Bruised.
Credit: ©Washington and Lee University 2016.

DOI: 10.4324/9780367824167-7

(THE SEDUCTIVE CUNNING OF) MUSIC   133

As mentioned in a few places previously, it is imperative to keep in mind the power of music. I am devoting this space to this topic because I feel that its influence is frequently underestimated. For young choreographers who may be searching for a place, a time period, a storyline, or emotion to root their work, music can feel like a savior. It is strong and structured and especially when one is flailing and perhaps feeling powerless amidst the many options or, most of the time, staring at a blank page or studio, it feels like a welcome, guiding hand.

What inexperienced choreographers sometimes don't realize is that music doesn't merely guide, it can dictate. It lulls us into feeling secure. Music can tell us where, how fast, and with what quality to move. It can tell us whether we are happy, carefree, sad, or lonely. It can shape our story or even change our meanings. It takes an experienced choreographer to stand up to this power. In seasoned hands, the power of music can be used to manipulate, to underscore the intent of the choreographer. Its driving eight-count beat, for example, can be turned on its head, disregarded, or purposefully underscored based on the needs of the maker. It takes someone who understands this power to deal with it effectively and use it for their purposes.

I don't allow new choreography students to use music. They create their homework assignments in silence, which I feel focuses them on the thematic work and keeps them safely away from outside influences. It's quite difficult for most of my choreography students to make work in silence. I think this may be the first inkling that they've possibly been relying too heavily on music in the past. They complain that they have no basis for what movements to choose or where to begin.

To help them find their way, I introduce my flowchart at the beginning of the term. This gives them guardrails that are geared toward thematic content creation without any undue influence from sources other than those the creator uses for research and development. Sometimes music is part of their research process. In such a case, I encourage them to listen to more than one piece by a certain composer or with a certain theme to broaden and widen their research so that they aren't relying solely on one piece.

In some cases, the students will get attached to a piece early on or use one piece exclusively for improvisation. In these cases, we've experimented with using the inspiring piece for improvisation experimentation but setting the work to something different. In one instance, a student and I were at an impasse because he loved a piece of music deeply and I felt strongly that it detracted from his composition and the development of his thematic material, so we compromised. This was in the days before cordless headphones, so we taped an iPod onto his hip and ran the cords (and more tape) up under his pants and shirt so they could sit in his ears almost invisibly. At the performance, he listened to it on headphones, and the audience experienced it in silence. (He was invited to perform it in the gala at American College Dance Festival that year.)

Slowly, over the course of the semester, we begin to play with sound, using text as music or crickets chirping, or wind chimes. Later we work with GarageBand to create and mix our own music or sound effects, and sometimes we are lucky enough to have live, improvised music. When we finally begin to integrate traditional music into making work, I first introduce exercises to help the students see its influencing nature.

I give my students an assignment to make a thirty-second dance about something specific of my choosing. It is usually something they can all relate to, like their first day of college. They tend to choose indirect and light movement that indicates nervousness or fear, some indicate a dreamlike state and some excitement. I ask them to perform their dances four times for one another with no explanation or introduction. The first and second piece of music I choose is the same for every student. The first piece is fun, fast tempo, and happy. The second piece is the opposite. For the third and fourth trials, I choose music at random from a wide variety of choices. This exercise is repeated for each student, and we chat afterward about how the music influenced the dancer as she performed and influenced the audiences' understanding of what they were seeing. We discuss the ways in which the students altered their perceptions of theme in regard to the first two renditions with contrasting accompaniment and in what ways, if any, the dancer was unconsciously influenced in performance.

At the end of the exercise, the dancer shares his/her/their thematic material, and we talk about this theme in relation to the various pieces of music. Usually, there are times when the music was a perfect accompaniment or perfect counterpoint to the choreography and many

(THE SEDUCTIVE CUNNING OF) MUSIC 135

times we saw a relationship between the two that was so layered or so delicate that it might have been impossible to plan for its arrangement in just that way. This is always an eye-opening experiment for new choreographers and helps to highlight the powerful role that music plays in dance.

An issue that comes up every year with new choreographers is lyrics in music. Young dancers and new choreographers love to use music that's either popular and/or has a singer. While I'd never question an experienced choreographer about this, and certainly I have used a lot of music of this sort, young choreographers generally use this type of music as an aid. They feel the communicative power of music and try to harness it to tell their story. I find myself asking my students, *What is the purpose of the dance if the music is already telling the story? Why make the dance if the story is being told in words? Why tell the composer's story?*

Part of the power of dance is communicating those things that defy words or explanation. Why use an alternate form of communication? Because it's easier? Maybe. It's vital to understand that choosing music with lyrics can augment an already precarious imbalance enough to derail the piece. There have been times in student showings when the dance is saying something contrary to the music, and I wonder what purpose it serves in speaking against it. The answer I usually received is that they like the beat of the music, so they ignore or dismiss the lyrics when choreographing. My response is that the scope of the music research needs to widen. Students many times feel that one particular beat is the only one that speaks to them when, in reality, there is a world of music waiting to be explored. Music from other countries, from other instruments, music libraries, and other sources is out there waiting to be discovered.

Having said all of this, there have been times when these little rules I created for my students were thrown away when a student had a sound, artistic reason why they wanted to do one or the other of these things, or they wanted music to be the inspiration for their work. That's great. If these issues are thought through, and if artistically sound choices are made with an open mind and can be backed up through discussion, I'm on board. As long as music isn't being used as a crutch or an easy communicative device, as long as it's a partner in the thematic goals,

136   (THE SEDUCTIVE CUNNING OF) MUSIC

as long as it's original, creative, and appropriate in some way, then the choreography is speaking.

Using sounds to forward thematic material is an opportunity to create your own sound *score*. Using music, environmental sounds, ring tones, or other noise and making them your own means you sample, edit, remix, and produce your own accompaniment. (Within reason. We'll discuss music copyright later.) What does it mean to take the "Star Spangled Banner" and edit silence over the music at ten-second intervals? How does it affect a dance work if Martin Luther King's "I Have a Dream" speech is overlaid on top of Common's rap "A Dream"? What if it's edited together with the sounds of a workers' strike rally or overlaid on top of jazz music, a movie score, or stand-up comedy? How do these things inform and reflect the thematic material of the piece? Why not take an opportunity to dance to text? I've seen a reset of Pearl Primus' *Strange Fruit* (set to the poem of the same name by Abel Meeropol published as Lewis Allan). Powerful doesn't describe it. But must choreography reflect and tell the same story as the text? Can it be a counterpoint? Can it tell its own story? I once set a dance to the breathing of the dancers by hooking them up with cordless microphones. They became their own accompaniment. Of course, silence is an option in its own right, and it can also be used eloquently as punctuation among a piece set to sound or music.

When my students are feeling devoid of ideas, I ask them to perform their phrases to music of my choosing. How does that change things? What if the dance you've been working on for three months and is a personal story of loss is performed to polka music? How is the music in communication with the movement? How is the movement in communication with the music? What if that same piece is performed again to an aria from *Eurydice*? How do we interpret the dance now? This never fails to open up new pathways of conversation, of inspiration, of clarity. We've experimented with this in performance as well. There have been times when we've used a certain piece or pieces of music in rehearsal and then performed to something completely different. I love this process because it never fails to create an interesting sense of dissonance with a few precious moments of harmony.

While it may read like music just took a beating under my tutelage, it can be an amazing partner. It can help you tell your story, serve as a buffer and act as a counterpoint. It can say one thing while the dance says another if you want to create tension, and a beautiful moment of power occurs when you can speak together in harmony. Riffing off of specific measures and breaking apart and rejoining tempos can be fulfilling as a choreographer and enable you to create crescendos in movement. Creating your own music or sound scores is also an opportunity to express your theme in more than one way. Two communicative devices piggybacking and supporting one another is exciting as long as it's truly a collaborative partnership.

7

INTELLECTUAL PROPERTY

Figure 7.1 This Macaroni and Cheese Crayon Tastes Like Wax.
Credit: ©Washington and Lee University 2016.

Music

No consideration of music is complete without discussing intellectual property. Just like the dance work you are creating is your property, so too is the music in the show (and the video/photo projection, costume design, lighting design, etc.) the property of the artist or artists who made it or those who own it. Just like all art forms, music is intrinsically valuable. When an artist makes work and shares it with the world, it must be protected from theft. I am not a lawyer, and this topic can get into the weeds very easily, so I will include below my experiences and what I've learned from requesting permissions for many years. This is by no means an exhaustive dive into copyright law but hopefully it will be a starting point for doing the right thing.

Music rights ensure that the musician, recording artist, and/or writer/composer are compensated for their work. Copyright law gives musicians the right to perform, distribute, reproduce, and adapt their own work and to give others permission to do so.[1] (These rights are slightly limited due to "fair use" clauses for educational and news reporting purposes, for example, among others. But for our purposes—university dance ticketed performances in which full songs are used—"fair use" will not come in to play.) ASCAP (American Society of Composers, Authors, and Publishers) BMI (Broadcast Music Incorporated), MPA (Music Publishers Association), and SESAC (originally the Society of European Stage Authors and Composers) are the four basic rights-holding companies. They exist to serve as an agent between artists who wrote/own music and people who want to play that music in public. For the right to use any music in their catalog, these companies will charge an annual fee that is based on the size of the organization, the number of performances offered, ticket prices, and the size of the theater (the number of seats). Then, based on a system that integrates song popularity with a number of uses, location, and a bunch of other factors, the company creates an algorithm that is used to pay the musicians.

Each of these companies has its own catalog of music that it covers. So, unless you know or plan to research exactly which company is holding the rights to the music you want to use, it's best to contract with all of them. It is possible to search the sites, so if you only need one piece of

140   INTELLECTUAL PROPERTY

music, you can find out who is holding the rights and pay only them. Be aware that these companies have spyware online and real-life employees who seek out performances that don't have proper music permissions, and can cause a lot of trouble. They will immediately involve their lawyers and send out "cease and desist letters," and should they go unheeded, won't hesitate to litigate. While this may seem litigious on the part of the companies, using music without proper permission is stealing. The music is the artists' work, and they both deserve to be compensated for that work and reserve the right to decide who can reproduce it.

It's important to note that the above information covers music that is played solely on its own. It covers music that you might play at intermission, for example, or pre-show. It can also cover music that's played in the studio while you are taking classes. It's a huge misconception that ASCAP, BMI, and the rest cover the rights of music that is accompanying a dance performance. For that, you need "grand rights." Grand rights are associated with any performance that is telling a story (or even just part of a story), has a theme or plot, or exists as an abstract movement. In other words, they are required whenever you layer something on top of a piece of music. Even when making abstract work, regardless of whether thematic material was intended, meaning is created.

For grand rights you must contact the publisher/music rights holder directly. This can be incredibly time-consuming as many times, the singer isn't the rights holder. You'll need to research the piece of music to see who wrote and published it, and you'll need to follow the trail if the rights have been sold or transferred to other(s). The Library of Congress's online music search as well as the US copyright registration records card catalog that is part of the US Copyright Office are great places to find information about music rights. This information may also be available through the search engines at the big four copyright holders mentioned above. Searching these sites will, at the very least, tell you who the publisher was and when the song was published. From there you can contact the publisher to inquire about the rights holder. It's a bit of detective work on your own. (If you are flush with cash, you can pay companies who will help you track down the owner of the copyright.)

Once you find the rights holder, the best approach is one email with a succinct description of who you are and where you are located. Email is best so that you have a record in writing of the conversation in case issues come up later. Also include what song(s) you'd like permission to use and why, the dates of the performance, the number of seats in the theater, and ticket prices. Start months and months ahead of time because, in my experience, they tend to ignore small venues with little influence or audience draw. I tend to send the email two or three more times over the next month or so to try to get their attention. Many times, when they realize I'm asking about a four-hundred-seat auditorium in the middle of southwest Virginia in a town of seven thousand, they give me permission to use the music as long as I credit the creator(s). (You must always credit the creators in the program whether you receive the music gratis or pay for it.) Sometimes, if the music is very popular, I may get a request for one hundred dollars.

One time a few years ago, I set my choreography to an old piece of music from the 1950s that, a few months after I started rehearsals, turned up in a hit movie. The song garnered a new life seventy years after it premiered, and it broke sales records. They asked me to pay five thousand dollars for the use of it! Needless to say, I reset my dance to something different. It was frustrating at the time, but I believe that a dance is the product of a very specific moment in time, and if that moment includes a sudden music change, then that's part of the process. Things like this give the dance a patina. They direct it down a new path, and it always, without fail, does something amazing to the dance that I never could have thought of or created on my own. I trust serendipity.

Just when you think you're up to the task, a further complication arises. As is the case for most small dance companies, if you plan on using recorded music, you have to get second permission. The grand rights will take care of permission to use the music, but you will also need to request permission to use a recorded version of that music. For this you must seek permission from the owner of the master recording. In many cases, this will be the publishing house but not always.[2] If your research for the music rights was deep enough, you should have collected this information along the way. Reach out to them in the same way you did to request the grand rights.

There are a couple of creative ways around dealing with intellectual property laws. One, which I love for more than just the freedom of not having to deal with legal ambiguities, is working with a musician or musicians to create new music for your piece or, better yet, to collaboratively work together and create the dance and music in tandem. This not only has the lovely outcome of paying musicians directly for their work, but it also stretches the mind and imagination of the choreographer (and musicians) through collaboration and brings a new piece of art into the world. This requires funding which, if organized in advance, can be garnered through grants, fundraising, and/or careful budgeting. A project of this sort would need to be organized well ahead of time anyway in order to give the musicians and the choreographer time to talk, create, work together, work separately, come back together, edit, organize, rehearse, etc. It takes time but is a wonderfully fruitful, collaborative adventure.

A simpler and more cost-effective measure is to use music in the public domain. The general rule (for music published in the United States) is that it is protected by copyright for the life of the composer plus seventy years (if the license wasn't renewed at some point). In other words, as of 2022, generally, if a piece of music was created before or during 1926, it is not protected by copyright.[3] Some music is in the common domain because it was never copyrighted, and some authors have donated their music for free use.[4] (If you plan to use music you think may be in the public domain, do your research. There are many exceptions to the general rules I mention above.)

In my experience, most students prefer not to use music with age because they feel it doesn't speak to them. After reading my chapter on music, I'm sure it's clear that I feel this is exactly why they should use it. As I previously mentioned, music is powerful, and my feeling is that if music doesn't have control over the choreographer, they can be better at their job. Another option is to encourage students to choreograph to music in the common domain but use something else for the performance. In this way, the music won't heavily influence their choreography and additionally, it won't matter if their chosen piece of music to perform to is rejected or a high fee is demanded because after rehearsing to something different, the music will end up being layered on top of the movement as opposed to being set to the movement. In this case, any piece of music would work. Obviously, you want to carefully choose music that has a relationship to the theme of the piece, however, ideally, the choreography isn't bound to the music. There's freedom in that.

INTELLECTUAL PROPERTY   143

A real-life example of this chapter's content is evident in this book's companion website. You will have noticed when you saw the "VIDEO REFERENCE" call out, and you clicked on the website and referenced link, that it contains a video of the choreography that has had its music removed. Although I obtained grand rights so that I could use each piece of music in performance, I did not obtain the streaming rights. Because what I am referencing is such a huge body of work that contains well over forty pieces of music, and because the publisher is a for-profit company and the author will receive royalties on sales of the book, the cost to obtain the streaming rights would have been astronomical. More importantly, as mentioned above, each individual rights holder would have to be researched, sought out, and contacted which would take an enormous amount of time, assuming that I ever heard back from them at all. This would have been impossible with the book deadlines. For these reasons, I included the videos with no sound but did link to the music so that one can listen to the music while watching the video. This ensures that the rights holders receive commissions. Interestingly, while writing

Figure 7.2 Wall Flowers/Wild Flowers.
Credit: ©Washington and Lee University 2022.

144 INTELLECTUAL PROPERTY

this book, I spoke with six different entertainment lawyers about this issue. None of them gave me any conclusive advice and they all expressed frustration with the vagaries of the law. However, in deference to the artists who made the work and out of an abundance of caution, I decided that this improvised system provides a great teaching moment.

Movement

It may seem that the laws surrounding the use of music are complex. To have a conversation about copyright in movement, you must multiply that complexity by one thousand. Part of the problem is that there is no set definition of what plagiarism in dance is or rules for standards of practice when sampling or borrowing ideas or phrases. It's all very vague and virtually uncontested in courts. Who's to say what the difference is between plagiarism and inspiration? Where is the line?

Prior to the mid- to late 1970s, video wasn't available to most people and definitely not affordable, so dance didn't really have a way to record itself except through handwritten notes, film, labanotation, or other complex or expensive systems. Dance wasn't even covered by copyright until 1976. Dance copyright now extends through the life of the creator plus fifty years, after which it becomes part of the public domain (with exceptions, of course.) With copyright came a definition of what was covered, and those guidelines are very similar to music. But no guidance was given on what constituted a violation.

There are a few very high-profile cases where one artist claims they borrowed or were inspired by another artist, but the creator claims material was stolen. Much like music and writing, I think the line lies somewhere in a balance between the amount of material, changes to the material, other designs present in the material, and attribution. The various elements are weighted according to importance. There's nuance involved.

I believe there is no hard and fast rule when it comes to plagiarism in dance because each case is unique. A general standard must be applied but measured by the details of each individual case. One must ask herself, how much of the work was replicated? Was it eight counts or three minutes of movement? Was it remade in exactly the same way as the original, or were there changes or adaptations so the work was presented

INTELLECTUAL PROPERTY 145

in a different manner? Was it made as an homage to the original? Was the original idea and owner credited? Were other parts of the dance taken as well, such as costumes, lighting, or camera angle?

There was an uproar in the dance world when Beyoncé's video to her song "Countdown" bore a remarkable similarity to world-renowned Belgian choreographer, Anne Teresa de Keersmaeker's *Rosas Danst Rosas* and, more abstractly, *Achterland*. To add insult to injury, elements of costume, lighting, and camera angles were also lifted from *Rosas Danst Rosas*. Beyoncé admitted that she looked to de Keersmaeker's work for inspiration but denied she stole anything. She claimed that she used these pieces of choreography among other inspirations and molded them to create something unique. Understandably, de Keersmaeker feels that not only was her work plagiarized but because of Beyoncé's presentational style, her dramatic and powerful thematic material was undercut and simplified.[5] Similar accusations arose when Beyoncé's "Run the World (Girls)" digital projection appeared to mimic Italian pop artist Lorella Cuccarini's projection and, again, when she released the video for "Single Ladies (Put A Ring On It)," and claimed she was "inspired" by Bob Fosse and his 1969 dance *Mexican Breakfast*.

At the 2018 Country Music Awards, Kelsea Ballerini performed "Miss Me More" set to choreography that was almost identical to Ohad Naharin's *Echad Mi Yodea*. By all accounts, both Naharin and de Keersmaeker were unbothered by the theft (although de Keersmaeker called it "rude"[6]). Brilliantly, both Naharin and de Keersmeaker used the crime to their advantage. Naharin used uproar in the dance community to plug his upcoming show where audiences could "come watch the real thing,"[7] and de Keersmaeker posted a challenge for companies to use *Rosas Danst Rosas* as inspiration and upload their versions of the dance to her website. She provided videos of her and one of her dancers, Samantha van Wissen, teaching the movement from each section in detail as well as directions for integrating the sections into the whole. She also shared her music and told choreographers that she "will teach you the moves, step by step, from the second part of the performance. After that it becomes your dance: *you dance Rosas*."[8]

De Keersmaeker's response inspired thousands of choreographers (including me) to rise to the challenge of using her work as inspiration and collectively celebrate the shared material. Clearly, in both of these cases, there's a much larger and deeper conversation here regarding power, race, politics, aesthetics, religion, commercial and art house dance, consumerism, and citation, among other things. I recommend delving into it.

I frequently use the examples mentioned above and show videos of each (there are many comparison videos on YouTube for viewing) to initiate a conversation in the classroom. The "web dance" challenge I mentioned earlier in the book is a great way for students to practice the difference between plagiarism and inspiration. Further, discussing this topic as a group keeps the issue of inspiration in the front of their minds as they research and rehearse for their classroom choreography assignments and, later, for performances.

Notes

1 "What Musicians Should Know about Copyright," United State Copyright Office, accessed September 4, 2022, https://www.copyright.gov/engage/musicians

2 Amelia Lukas, "Music Licensing 101: The Pretty to the Nitty-gritty," Dance/USA, September 14, 2012, https://www.danceusa.org/ejournal/2012/09/14/music-licensing-101-the-pretty-to-the-nitty-gritty

3 "When Does Music Become Public Domain?" Cloud Cover Media, accessed September 4, 2022, https://cloudcovermusic.com/music-licensing-guide/when-does-music-become-public-domain

4 Rich Stim, "The Public Domain," Nolo, with much taken from *Getting Permission: Using and Licensing Copyright-Protected Materials Online and Off*, Berkeley, CA: Nolo, 2019, https://fairuse.stanford.edu/overview/public-domain

5 James McKinley, Jr., "Beyoncé Accused of Plagiarism Over Video," *The New York Times*, October 10, 2011, https://archive.nytimes.com/artsbeat.blogs.nytimes.com/2011/10/10/beyonce-accused-of-plagiarism-over-video

6 Ibid.

7 Lauren Wingenroth, "Can Music Artists Stop Stealing from Choreographers Already?" *Dance Magazine*, November 18, 2018, https://www.dancemagazine.com/can-music-artists-stop-stealing-from-choreographers-already

8 "Re: Rosas, The fABULEUS Remix Project" (website), accessed September 4, 2022, https://www.rosasdanstrosas.be/en-home

8

ADVICE

Figure 8.1 Student dancer in performance.
Credit: ©Washington and Lee University 2010.

148   ADVICE

In the thirty-five years since I first started choreographing and teaching dancers, and later, teaching students to choreograph, I've come to understand general problems and fears associated with composition and a few methods for helping people get back on track. I think the biggest issue college students face is akin to writer's block. You stand in the middle of a huge empty dance studio, looking at yourselves in mirrors, iPhone at the ready for playing music, and you freak out. The fact that you have seemingly a zillion choices is paralyzing. You may feel there's too much space, too many options, too much pressure (and/or little time). You may feel as if you've said all you can with your body or that you don't have anything original to offer. A secondary issue related to this one, and many times a result of this one, occurs when, out of desperation for material, the choreographer starts repeating themself. They reuse old phrases or string together "comfortable" movements. By that I mean movement that feels good on their body, is familiar, isn't necessarily challenging, and perhaps looks tired or obsolete or, maybe even worse, derivative of someone else's work. Reaching back to old ways of moving may enable a choreographer to quickly string together movement but it is basically just plagiarizing oneself. It really can be debilitating for young choreographers. Below are a few suggestions I offer to help you get back on track.

1. **Start with something.** This something can be something tangible like a book, a group of photos, a journal to write in, props that are interesting, etc. You could bring in tools with which to make the "something." Scissors, magazines, glue, white sheets and markers, or five-foot-wide paper rolls and crayons can help to spark the imagination. "Found" materials are great tools for this as well. What's in your kitchen that you can bring? On the floor of your car? In your backpack? Sit down with your items and begin to work. If you don't yet have any thematic material, just start working with no objective in mind. Draw, paint, sculpt. Make two-dimensional and three-dimensional work. Let your mind wander as you work. Note how the materials feel, how they look, what shapes they make. Rip them up and put them together in a new way. Look at them upside down and bottom right diagonal to top left. Record yourself speaking. Write in the journal. Cut the photos apart and make a new shape with them. Read about others' work. Read dance reviews in *The New York Times*, the *Village Voice*, or *The Guardian*. It not

ADVICE 149

Figure 8.2 M(other).
Credit: ©Washington and Lee University 2016.

150 ADVICE

only keeps you up-to-date on what is going on in the dance world, but it envelops you in the vocabulary and terminology of the field. Specific word usage can be an indicator of what's just below the surface of the dance work. Learning how to speak and write about dance influences your perception of what you're making. Reading about works you haven't seen creates mental images, shapes, and inspiration even if you've never seen one step of the work. Be aware that, although someone well versed in dance is writing the review, it still is just one person's opinion seen through a specific lens.

2. **Do something with the something**. Once you have your research materials, if you have a theme, emotion, or story in mind, try to find connections to what you're making. If you've come in with an open mind to whatever is presented to you, look at form, shape, line, texture, color, and let it inspire you. How can you transpose onto your body the images, patterns, and shapes from writing and the lines from drawing? Must the transposition always be on the arms and legs? How does making a triangle with your shoulders look? Can you make the angle of a martini glass using your head? Transpose shapes onto unlikely parts of the body. Journaling contains not only the shapes made by the words but the meaning of them. How does writing about the wedding of your sister make you feel? Can that be danced? Do the curves of your cursive journal writing add a nuance to your movement? How can these two elements coalesce? What if this coalesced movement was danced by your rib cage or, to come back to the theme, danced by your ring finger on your left hand? Dance your material forwards and backward, with your head and with your toe, laying on your back, standing on your head. Based on my earlier warnings about music, it may seem funny that I mention it here but music as inspiration is very different than setting dance to a specific piece of music that inspires you. If your thematic material is about joy and you find various pieces of music that make you feel joy, use improvisation to those pieces as source material. Just be careful about setting the entire piece to that music. Resist the urge!

3. **Record the something**. Even if all you're doing is playing around, video yourself. When you're actively making work in the studio, you are usually playing the role of a dancer. All of the examples in #2 above, if recorded, could be looked at and analyzed from the point of

view of an observer. Watching recordings of movement shifts your perspective, which can be helpful. Recordings are also very valuable tools if your method of inspiration is improvisation. Dancers can get caught up in improv and it may morph from one thing into another throughout the course of the improvisation. Recording all of it will give you the opportunity to choose which pieces you like and want to keep and which to forgo. Joyful music will cause you to move in joyful ways. If that's your goal, fill your phone with twenty pieces of music that make you feel that way. You can use the improvisation from those pieces as a vocabulary with which to sculpt your work. Many times, choreographers will involve their dancers in the improvisational phase. They will encourage involvement and suggestions from their cast and implement a variety of ideas into the piece. This is one way to ensure that you aren't accidentally repeating or borrowing from yourself. Some dancers like contributing in this way better than others. In my experience, this is usually because they have little experience working in this way and feel shy to do so. Improvisation is a learned skill. If you've never taken an improvisation class, do it. For choreographers who want to work in this way, please, PLEASE give credit to your dancers as co-collaborators. Do not use them as free labor. Be aware as you do so, though, that this has legal implications. Co-creators, in most cases, have the right to reset the work without permission. Read up on dance rights for joint ownership in dance works.

4. **Keep making something**. Even if you think it's terrible, even if you hate it, keep pushing. Try not to judge your work. Just let it be the work. Keep your opinions out of the studio. Keep creating, and through the process of doing, recording, watching, and editing, it will slowly start to be something. It may be painfully slow, and you may want to give up but, in the making, there will eventually be a breakthrough. Don't stop creating. Don't judge what you create. Just create.

5. **Edit the something**. Don't be afraid to remove large chunks. No movement is precious. As earlier, I mention Doris Humphrey's quote "All dances are too long."[1] Dance it in reverse order. Dance it on your right arm. Cut out parts and move them around. This is where using iMovie or other video programs will aid you. It makes the dance tangible, which gives you the freedom split it into pieces so they can be moved around or discarded at will. Dance is ephemeral. If you

152   ADVICE

become a perfectionist, you create concrete walls around yourself. One must bravely edit with abandon.

6. **Show your something**. Show it over and over, even if you only have twenty seconds of material. Show it to everyone, not just dancers or dance teachers. This will give you a variety of opinions and feedback from diverse sources with differing histories and experiences. Try to discover how it makes them feel, if it's challenging in some way if it elicits thoughts, ideas, or story. I'm not suggesting that the choreographer change anything based on these responses, but hearing how people are viewing it can further inspire or encourage one to look more deeply at the work or down a new path. It may present questions the choreographer hadn't considered before. What I'm not suggesting is finding out if others "like" it or not. That's irrelevant and subjective. What you want to discover is its impact.

7. **Have fun with the something**. As hard as it is, try not to take the creation of choreography too seriously. If your dance isn't exactly what you want it to be, is that really so terrible? While I respect dance because I see what it gives to society, how it heals, and what is grown from its seeds, I also realize that all artists have choreo-block at times. We all struggle. We all have produced work that we later wish we hadn't. The key is to learn from these experiences and know that you might possibly fail but try anyway. There was an old insurance commercial thirty years ago whose tagline was something like, "The greatest risk is not taking one."[2] I think that applies in such a lovely way to dance. Dance exists on the edge of failure. That's part of what's so exciting about it.

8. **Don't be afraid to circle back to the beginning and start with something new**. It doesn't mean you are starting over. You've amassed material and kinesthetic knowledge and experience in the preceding steps. You are simply circling back in the same way that we do within the choreographic flowchart and applying new knowledge to original inspiration and questioning where you are and what is meaningful to you. It may help to "unstick" you mentally/creatively to go through another round of inspiration. I've found when working with college students that they take great interest in and relate to the work of alums of our dance program. Following this is a collage of visual art created by dancer/ artist alums of the college where I teach. These works and others have independently jump-started the creative focus of my current students.

ADVICE 153

Figure 8.3 (Top left) Screenshot of video, *MASCCHAOS*, Elliot Reza Emadian, video, 2021. (Top right) Painting, *Rhythm I*, Emily Danzig, acrylic paint, 2022. (Middle left) *Koi in a Storm*, Irina Koleva, acrylic on canvas, 2019. (Bottom left) Mixed Media, *Cathexis*, Sara Dotterer, acrylic paint and collage, 2019. (Bottom right) *Untitled*, Lisa Stoiser, digital illustration (procreate), 2019.

Credit: (Top left) Courtesy of Elliot Reza Emadian. (Top right) Courtesy of Emily Danzig. (Middle left) Courtesy of Irina Koleva. (Bottom left) Courtesy of Sara Dotterer. (Bottom right) Courtesy of Lisa Stoiser.

Notes

1 Doris Humphrey, *The Art of Making Dances* (New York: Rinehart, 1959; Princeton: Princeton Book Company 1991).
2 "Rethinking Risk," *Forbes*, December 4, 2002, https://www.forbes.com/2002/12/04/cx_aw_1204risk.html?sh=6995ff1b442b

9
A CONVERSATION AMONG ARTISTS

Figure 9.1 La Fenêtre.
Credit: ©Washington and Lee University 2017.

DOI: 10.4324/9780367824167-10

156 A CONVERSATION AMONG ARTISTS

I can see that it could be difficult to make sense of all of the material in this book. While I feel like my flowchart will help new choreographers as a set of crutches, aiding them as they find their way, it can be challenging to navigate one's own style and sense of choreography. Processes and methodology are personal, and I imagine no two choreographers work in exactly the same way. For this reason, I thought it might be helpful to be a part of a conversation between myself and three other choreographers as we discuss our approaches toward the art form and our techniques used when making work.

These three artists are longtime friends of mine. During Covid, we had a group Zoom where we discussed what composition means to us, how we approach it, and the ways in which the process revealed and taught us about ourselves and how we make work. I recorded our conversation. What follows is a transcript. It's my hope that by reading about four very different ways of working, the reader will not only come to understand the many and varied processes that exist but will also feel confident in experimenting with and developing their own.

First, an introduction to my guests:

> **ShaLeigh Comerford** is an Irish & Native American choreographer and the artistic director of ShaLeigh Dance Works, a dance-theater company based in Durham, NC, and founded in 2005. She is a graduate of Hollins University with a master's degree in Visual and Performing Arts. ShaLeigh began her formal dance training on scholarship with the Roanoke Ballet Theatre and the American Dance Festival and continued her training in NYC and at P.A.R.T.S in Brussels, Belgium. In 2011, she trained in the Gaga movement language with Ohad Naharin and the Batsheva Dance Company in Tel Aviv, Israel. ShaLeigh apprenticed with the Bill T. Jones/Arnie Zane Dance Company and has performed with Keigwin & Company, Tina Croll & Company, the Dendy Dance Theater, Carolina Ballet, Martha Clarke, Rosie Herrera, an Official Music Video for "Blind" by Christian Löffler, as well as with Washington and Lee University in a restaging of Batsheva's Minus Sixteen.

> **Liza Deck** earned her MFA in dance from Arizona State University after attending Hope College where she received the Florence Cavanaugh Dance Award. She has performed professionally with Andrew's Arts Dance Company, Aerial Dance Company, Roanoke Ballet Theatre,

A CONVERSATION AMONG ARTISTS   157

Opera Roanoke, Mill Mountain Theatre, danah bella dance works and is currently the head of City Modern Ensemble. Since 1994, Mrs. Deck has directed the Fleming-Ruffner dance department and is proud to be the founder of the F.R.E.E. Dance Company. Liza has taught at the American College Dance Festival, Regional High School Dance Festival, Hollins outreach, Virginia Tech outreach, and Washington and Lee University. Her choreography has been featured/she guest performed at Virginia Tech, Radford University, Hollins University, and Washington and Lee University.

Sandra Meythaler *was a principal ballerina with the National Ballet of Ecuador. She has performed ballet and contemporary dance around the world including Peru, Belgium, Germany, Italy, England, France, Spain, Brazil, Columbia, and Japan. She began dancing professionally at the age of fifteen with Compania Nacional de Dance in Ecuador and then joined the National Ballet of Ecuador in 1989. She also danced with Ballet Novo, Opera Ecuador, and Koral y Esmeralda. In 2001 Sandra became a part of Roanoke Ballet Theatre and was promoted to Executive Director in 2007. She is also an adjunct professor of dance at Washington and Lee University. Ms. Meythaler's awards include Silver Medal—Festival International de Dance—Dijon, France, Bronze Medal—Festival de Dance—Castrovillari, Italy Best Performance—Festival International de Dance—Tarascon, France—Nominated Best Interpretation—Festival of Choreography—Ecuador, Award given by Hitoshi Motochino, Mayor Nagasaki, Gold Medal—Awarded by Organization MINON, Tokyo.*

Jenny: The act of creating is part of who I am. There isn't a separation between my life and my work. It's the same system. One informs the other and they speak and interact. It's a conversation. The things that frustrate me, challenge me, and inspire me are worked through in real time in my life and in my art. I think that's part of the reason I consider the act of composition such an intimate experience. Can you talk a bit about your choreographic process in terms of inspiration?

Liza: I am driven by a force outside of myself. It's in me and it has to get out. All the ideas have to be out there in the world, not just written in my notes or performed by myself. Somebody else has to do it. I don't care if the audience sees it. I just have to get it out there on dancers.

ShaLeigh: I feel that way too. Ever since I started creating, there's been this kind of trend where I get my idea for the next project while I'm in the middle of making the first one, and then it stays with me like an itch that has to be scratched. It's like Liza was saying, it's like feeling compelled even beyond the fear (because every time I start a new work, I feel like— what the hell am I doing?) I remember feeling so inspired when I finally learned that Pina Bausch felt the same way too, before making a work, or that Fellini made 8 1/2 while he was enduring writer's block. I pull on those things. Like Martha Graham said, "It's not your business to determine how good it is. It's your business to get it out into the world." I lean on that as a support because I equally want to do it and feel afraid of it at the same time. But it's something that just kind of has to exist.

Sandra: For me, I guess in the beginning, I needed to find a place to put all my love for dance because, from the time I can remember, I wanted to be a dancer. I danced for many years professionally but, when I started to age, there was a desperation of questioning who I am. I was a dancer but then suddenly I had to stop. I didn't know if there could be love for dance anymore in me. That was a kind of difficult time. Choreographing gave me the freedom to express what I feel and have this outlet, which allowed me to do something with all this love. I found choreography and teaching and began to fall in love again. Sometimes it's something that I need to do. Sometimes it's a job that I have to do. Sometimes I need to create because it's inside of me, and that is what I feel is a pure creation. All this love, technique, experience, and inspiration is going to give you what you need to make dance pieces. This sounds silly but it was true; I had surgery I don't remember how long ago. I tore my meniscus. I have a little bit of claustrophobia and you need to go into the machine to do the MRI. The noise is horrible, and I could not handle it. I got in and I closed my eyes. They played music inside and, in order to calm myself down, I choreographed in my head to these weird songs. It seemed like in a second it was over! (laughs) You can find inspiration anywhere. I feel the whole planet is a piece of art and you'll find art in every single thing there is around. That is what moves me.

ShaLeigh: Beautiful. You know, it's funny because while Sandra was talking about all of these different sources of inspiration, it totally took me all the way back to childhood. And I don't even know if I can really answer

A CONVERSATION AMONG ARTISTS   159

the question of why I create because I created my first choreography in first grade for the talent show. It was a ballet duet. I started making work both in dance and theater with my siblings from the time I was a kid. And I don't really know where that came from other than maybe a desire to create more beautiful worlds or a desire to create experiences for others and a desire to, I don't know, create a bunch of little snow globes that people can enter into, you know? To experience the wonder and the magic of the world. I think I always wished people could see the way I see the world, and I wish I could give them an experience like that. Like, if everyone in the world could suddenly be your best friend, and everyone in the audience, too, maybe they could see it. Yeah, I don't know. I think if I wasn't a big sister, maybe I wouldn't be a choreographer, you know?

Jenny: It sounds like dance is something that's innately part of all of you. You have to express yourself and, it doesn't matter if there are people who are buying tickets and watching you or not, because it's something that's so integral to who you are as a human. I think that's a fascinating thing about our field because you don't expect to hear an investment banker, for example, say, "It's so much a part of me. I deeply desire to facilitate mergers. I would do it even if no one paid me" (laughs). There's a level of intimacy here, I think, and it sounds like, for all of you, the need to create is part of who you are.

Sandra: It's something that I kind of questioned in myself sometimes. It's probably something that you are born with, because, from the time I have memory I was dressing up with whatever my mom had and standing up on the table, dancing. I charged my aunts money to watch me dance. (laughs) I was businesswoman then too! My mom used to say that of all her kids (she has six) I'm the only one who would look outside for hours while it was raining. Just looking. All kids have imaginations but, I feel like we didn't lose that when we grew up. Sometimes even now, you know, I'm all grown up and you sometimes see a beautiful sunset and it touches something inside of you and in that moment, I'm thinking, "Is everybody thinking and feeling the same way I feel?" Do they look at life in the same way we do? Is that why we become artists? I wonder, "How do the lawyers see it?" Life is life, you know, some pain and suffering and sometimes, happiness. And I feel like if I was not an artist, I don't know how I would live, because it's the only thing that pulls me out and in bad times. Because horrible things can be happening sometimes, and I put music on and move and one hour passed. I really enjoy it, you know, that moment of thinking nothing. I'll always stop on the middle (of my drive home) on the Natural Bridge and have a coffee there ... and then it is three hours later and I'm late for my other job. (laughs) I think we're weird. Or we are the normal ones? I don't know.

Liza: I know everybody has feelings and emotions and are affected by things but, growing up, that would happen to me all the time. I'd be looking outside, for example, and it wasn't especially beautiful, but there was something happening with the color and the light. And my brother Mike and my little sister would be like, "We gotta go, Liza. We're going to town" and my big brother Ben would say, "Stop, shh, she's doing stuff" and he would shut everybody out because I was doing something. This is interesting because he's a music composer. So, I don't know if he was maybe feeling it too? In these moments, I'm not just someone with my jaw going slack and my eyes unfocused going off to dreamland. I'm actually doing something actively, doing something important in nature and science. It really has inspired me over the years, and even now, I find that I use science in my work. I'll choreograph a piece based on a comet, for example. That's my inspiration. But if you looked at it and you listen to the music, you might think it's a piece about witches kidnapping a child. (laughs) I don't care that you didn't get my intent from it or that the thematic material came into me one way and then it came out as something different for you. That's how I choreograph. It doesn't matter if anyone out there understands my inspiration. I don't need a storyline. No offense to musicals. They're fabulous. (laughs) But I'm not required to tell a story or further the story in a specific way, which is freeing and another reason I don't make a lot of money. (laughs)

Jenny: I think for young choreographers, that's something that is hard for them to understand. I think that they feel like they failed if the audience doesn't completely understand what they're trying to say. They don't understand that every audience member is coming to the theater with a specific history, their own biases, a filter. They have a lens very specific to them. Audiences guessing your theme or intent isn't the point. We want them to interpret what we're doing in their own way.

A CONVERSATION AMONG ARTISTS 161

Liza: Yeah, I like it when they've got their own story or emotional response to my work. I enjoy it. I love hearing what it means to somebody else, and it being totally different from my intent. I like it when I start choreographing with one idea, and then another idea comes along. This harks back to what ShaLeigh said about her next dance coming out while she's working on the first. Sometimes I let that next dance take over the first dance, and the piece morphs as I'm going along. To me, it ends up being this beautiful, perfect creation. Now, I don't know if other people want to see it or if it is interesting to them, but it is to me.

Jenny: So, Liza, you said that science inspires you as does art and beauty. What else? Can you all talk about what else inspires you?

Liza: Kind of everything! Space and science and nature, other people's poetry, books, historical information, music—really a lot. Everything can be a dance for me. You could throw, you know, just throw some bananas, some half-eaten bananas and ... I think I must be hungry (laughs), but you can throw anything at me like that and I'd come up with some good ideas- or at least ideas I can't avoid. (laughs) Jenny, you've given me storylines and topics that I have to make choreography about. I'll just go research it. I remember there was this country song. *sings* "Hang from the highest tree"... But anyway, I researched the crap out of that. I looked at pictures of cowboys, the clothes they're wearing, different saloons, and different photographs of how they're holding a cigarette, for example. The end product might not have shown the layers and layers of research I put into it, but it informed the dance and the dancers. That's how I make being given a project fun. And I appreciate it because you've given me all kinds of opportunity. And it always expands my mind. Like when you were talking about performing an entire concert to live bluegrass music. You were like "We're doing a concert of all bluegrass music." And I'm like, "I have another thing to work on" and you're like, "No, I mean, I'd like us all to set work to bluegrass music." It's like, "Oh, okay. We're doing this. Okay. Yes, ma'am. Yes, ma'am" (laughs). But that was good! It takes me out of my little floating-in-the-space choreography ideas and challenges me.

ShaLeigh: I feel like my inspirations tend to be centered around people and their stories. And I will kind of have an idea that I might want to explore,

162 A CONVERSATION AMONG ARTISTS

but I'll always abandon it and bring the process, the inquiry, into the studio. And I think that what I really love doing is, looking at it as like an excavation site. And then I kind of see how the other dancers in the room respond to it. So, I really enjoy giving people opportunities. I feel like the process for me is as important, maybe more important in some ways, than the final result. I was asked a question once "How does your goal—what it is that you want to do, what you want to create—How does that inform your process?" And that was such an important question for me then, because I was still young, I had just moved to New York and, I didn't know what I was doing. I was kind of moving in a linear direction of like, you know, how I wanted to—what I wanted to kind of express. And when I started realizing that I wanted that to reflect back on the process. I think that my work has been process-based ever since. I would create a completely different work if different people were in the room with me when it was being made, which makes it really, really hard to do repertory kind of work. If I get opportunities to recreate an old work again, I don't really enjoy that. And I don't, you know, I feel like it doesn't pay tribute to the creators of it. I've only been asked to do that like a handful of times, so I haven't really had a chance to master it or anything. But I never really knew how to bring people deeper into the depths when they're learning it from the outside-in rather than creating it from the inside-out. But I feel like my work just tends to really center people and, at the end of the day, I don't want people to see dancers in my work, I want people to see people. And to like, maybe similarly, like to what Liza was saying, I don't feel any need to remove their agency or their autonomy as viewers. I love that if they find something that resonates. There's only a handful of emotions, but we can share that even if our stories are different. I really love that about the creative process, so I just feel like the humanity and trying to make sense of it all and dealing with the struggles that we all have, and the otherness that we all experience and the separation that we all experience. I'm really interested in those gaps, sharing vulnerability, sharing our own personal truths. And so yeah, I might have my own personal ideas, but when I come into a process, I'm really inspired by the people I'm working with.

Jenny: In my composition class the other day we were watching an interview with Mark Morris, and another with Twyla Tharp, and a few other people. The thing that tied all the people together was they said that, in

A CONVERSATION AMONG ARTISTS   163

certain instances or in the making of a specific work, they may walk into the studio with nothing prepared. And then they just work with the dancers in that moment. And some of the students were asking me how they start. How do you begin if you go in there with nothing? They felt they couldn't relate to that process. I'm sure maybe it differs from project to project and how prepared you may or may not be. Can you all talk about that, in general? How do you like to work when you're creating something brand new?

Sandra: For me, for example, the process is different depending on what is the show. For example, if we are doing a small black box, I bring the music and, like ShaLeigh said, I have an idea and motivation, and in the moment, I begin to listen to music. These ideas are beginning to come and are beginning to feed from the energy and what the dancers are doing in the moment. But also, I'm respecting my line of movement and how I like to move and translate. Sometimes I change my lines and adapt them to what the dancers are doing because I have something in my mind but, if it's not looking the way I want it to look on that specific dancer, then I adjust and listen to the dancer's body, and it becomes beautiful because it's them, not me, in there. Of course, if we're going to do *A Midsummer Night's Dream*, for example, that means this is the phrase of music I have and I spend time by myself in the studio, listening to the music, counting for them and beginning to divide the parts. This is a different process. I have my notebook and I listen and divide the music in sections. I write the script of the ballet first, the characters, and then I decide order of the program. I am beginning to have all these ideas of what is happening because I need to express the story to the audience. *A Midsummer Night's Dream* was based on the play, of course, but it was my choreography from the beginning to the ending. I was very well prepared. I studied, I read, I investigated, I write down notes. I even drew pictures. I cannot explain sometimes and have difficulty with language. English is my second language so I try to explain what I want from the pictures. When I draw in the book, I can explain better.

Liza: I prepare a lot of stuff at home. Not necessarily by standing up or moving, but I end up writing a lot of ideas down. I get kind of obsessed with whatever project I'm working on. I do come to rehearsals very prepared. This is useful because, you know, time is of the essence when dealing with my high school students. For my professional company, I might not prepare anything. We work together. A lot of people have ideas, a lot of people want to work, and I want my dancers to participate in the choreography. Music doesn't usually come first for me, but when I find a piece of music, I make a musical map too, like Sandra, and that really helps me prepare my ideas and kind of helps them coalesce. But I do my best work, I think, when I come into the studio with nothing but a little dream in my heart and then I started moving. (laughs) And it makes a difference who your dancers are at that moment too. If they're going to flow with you on that, if they're going to be patient, and if they're going to put some love into it. That's very important. It doesn't happen very often, but I have occasionally had a group who act like blocks of clay waiting for me to mold them, and I say, "You're going to have to mold yourself. You gotta move. I'm not going to place you exactly where you need to be." I find that, when I'm just coming in with a dream, I'm very up close to the dancers. Instead of seeing the big picture, I'm seeing their small movements and how their bodies interact with the bodies around them. It's very close. I don't know what that's about. But yeah, I'd have to say I both prepare a lot and also fly by the seat of my pants, and I'm inspired by what they're doing, all at the same time.

Sandra: Something Liza said has happened to me. She said that she doesn't want people to be blocks of clay and that she needs them to move. Sometimes, I need that too. That is one of the difficult things that I encounter in my job. Sometimes when I need to set a contemporary piece, you know, the company has twenty dancers and I choose five. I prepare a couple of phrases that give the dancers a lot of freedom. This always turns out best. Because the same choreography with different dancers is a completely different work. Sometimes I think to myself, "Oh my God, I need to give them the material spoon by spoon," and I think, "You need to give me something!" But, you know, not all the dancers are the same quality of artists. Some of them are, you know, incredible. Some of the dancers are extremely creative. And that makes me think they are in a long-term relationship with choreography. Others will be movers only and they don't have the imagination of what they can give into the choreography. They are expecting you to give them every second of movement, and that is difficult to work with. But I need to work with both, you know. It's very hard.

ShaLeigh: Yeah, I feel like I definitely have that too. One of the reasons I decided to start a company was because, the more you can train together and move together and build your aesthetic language together, then the easier it is to create. And then you have dancers that can express your ideas and their ideas at the same time. It's like you're sharing that language. But when you have change overs, and maybe new people coming in that haven't developed those skill sets yet, you are asked of a lot more as a choreographer. You have to be more of a director. My favorite way to work is more as a collaborator. So, I rarely like to set movement on dancers, unless these are dancers that have been working with me for a really long time, and I know that they're going to take what I give and amplify it. They're going to live inside of it. It's going to look like their movement. But when I do that with people who I haven't spent a lot of time with, it looks like someone taking on another skin and it stops speaking as a language. When I go into the studio, it just depends on how much time I have. I will say that I made a piece that lasted from 2007 to 2015 and it was definitely the dance I spent the most time on. (laughs) Every day I went home, and I was taking notes from our video and I was going in with new ideas and a response to what we had done the weekend or rehearsal before. I have a notebook for every single show that I do, and that's where all my ideas and tasks lists go, everything lives there. When I'm making evening length works, it's a little bit scarier, especially as someone who self produces. It depends on who is in the room. Are you going to be a collaborator today? Or are you going to have to direct today to help get people motivated to participate and to dive in? And then sometimes, if this particular piece that I'm working on right now has the biggest production crew I've ever worked with, like sound designer, composer, lighting designer, costume designer, props master, tech designer, the co-director, rehearsal director, people that are co-creators with us and then the company, I have to go in there now with set things to play with. And it feels a little bit prescribed. I'm not totally loving it. And I'm also wondering if because it's so big, there's that fear of letting go of control when you have so many different moving parts.

So, I just feel like every situation is so different, and it really asks of you to meet it in a completely different way. And sometimes, in an ideal world, you get to go in there with your top five dancers, and you get to really breathe together and experience and create together. But sometimes you have to go in there with your notes and starting places because other people aren't at the place where they can bring that yet. One of the pieces that felt the most satisfying to create was the one that I was able to invest in more fully ... and I don't know if other artists feel that way, but if I could live and eat and breathe a piece of work without dealing with administration and grants and taxes and board meetings and all that stuff, I would do that. That's all I want. I mean, I would prepare to the high heavens.

Jenny: It's interesting to hear you all talk about your approach. One of the things that's incredibly clear from hearing y'all talk is that you have to be mentally flexible and willing to change up your personal artistic processes. You may not be able to employ the tools you feel contribute to a successful piece if you are with people who are unable to work that way. So, there's this whole other level of artistic virtuosity at play. All of you are able to shift, reassess, and make your work in a different way based on whatever kind of situation is coming at you.

ShaLeigh: That's why we drink! (laughs) Okay, let's just be honest. (laughs)

Jenny: One of the things that I talk about in the book (and the reason I write about it is because it's always a huge topic of conversation not only in my composition class, but also in the dance company when students are making work) is the relationship of young choreographers to music. It's human nature to move when you hear music. It is deep in our bones and can happen without use even realizing it. Music can inspire how we move and the choices that we make. It's so powerful. So, when I'm working with my dancers, one of the things I ask them to do, which they *hate*, is choreograph without music. Make the piece in silence. Really, it's interesting to me ... I don't know, the psychology of music or its relationship to the human brain, but it's interesting to me how much this assignment freaks them out. Music is powerful in their lives.

A CONVERSATION AMONG ARTISTS 167

And, clearly, when you're an experienced artist like the three of you, that's something that you take into consideration, and you make choices. You decide whether you're going to let the music be an inspiration for your piece, whether you're going to use the music to forward your thematic material in some way or if the two are having a conversation, a fight, or have no relationship whatsoever. Some students don't really have the ability to parse this issue or make those choices yet. So, I'd love for you all to talk about your relationship to music.

Liza: Well, scientists can correct me, but my understanding is that when you hear sound, it hits your nervous system sooner than sight or touch or any other sense. So, you know when you hear a loud noise you like, "Ah!!" You freak out, even though, it's your husband right over there and he just dropped a model train. Your brain is not afraid, but your body says, "Loud noise, run away!" Music is very powerful, and it expresses so many things we all think and feel. It brings people together. Music can really bring people together. Having said that, music is not the thing that I choreograph to. If a song is playing, a full blown, fully figured-out piece of choreography floats along in my mind. It's complete. The whole thing is done already. I didn't research anything. That is not telling my story. The whole thing is choreographed already by the music. So, I think that I certainly can choreograph to music, but I would rather choreograph without music at all or, if a song is the inspiration, I change the music once it comes to setting the piece on others or performing the piece. It's going to be a completely different piece of music or something original I had somebody make for me based on my dance, which was based on another piece of music.

Sandra: For me, for example, we are doing this black box series, and we invited dancers from the company to create their own pieces. The exercise I like to do with them is that I put on one music, and then I tell them to do a phrase. And I truly believe that movement is just beautiful as movement if your goal isn't to communicate something specific. Then I say, "Okay, we change the whole music." But the problem is the movement may not go with that new music. I show that I can put exactly the same phrase with completely different music. You adjust the tempo, the spacing but, in the end, it is the same basic phrase. You can put intention in the movement in a different way. For me, it's okay that this music is my inspiration. Sometimes I need to find what I want to say. The choreography process is extremely deep, depending on what it is you want to say and what you're working with in that time.

ShaLeigh: One of the things that I used to do is this: if music gave me the inspiration for movement, I would record it, and I would record myself dancing to it. Then, I would watch it in silence. And I would ask myself if my movements still spoke. Was it only powerful because of the sound? Because then it's like the dance is actually serving the art form of music. If the music is what was making it powerful, then the dance is not speaking. I know that students fall in love with a song because it's so powerful. They choreograph to that song, and they don't realize that they're serving the song. They're not serving our art form of dance. And I really am in love with the interface between movement and music and something that can work more as like a collaboration, like the music is another dancer in the space. The way that the movement and the dance actually start to work together is a whole new dynamic, and you start to realize that when you switch up the music. Something that I learned early on just from having to edit all of my own work and create my own trailers and submit to applications and stuff was playing with things like, "What would that look like with this sound?" It just starts to tell an entirely different environmental story, because I feel like that's what sound does for me: it creates an environment, and it elicits different emotions. There's an entire context and a subtext that's happening in all of this information. So, it can deepen or distract. And those can be used as devices too. I love working with musicians and composers, and I love sharing with them. It's also interesting to me to find that kind of language between the two art forms to communicate ideas that you have. Yeah, I think it's a really beautiful, complex relationship, and I feel like it's so important that they're in dialogue with each other, as opposed to one layered on top of the other like a surface, because it just changes everything. It can really deepen the experience of being in a theater and watching dance or being in a site-specific space experiencing sound. Your senses are homed in from the things that you see to the things that you hear and, like Liza was saying, how it's connected to our nervous system. And when we start to work more with composers and environments, we start to realize that we're either soothing them into this experience, or we're giving them something loud to pull their attention. We are guiding the experience of our viewers, whether we're conscious of it or not.

Liza: It's interesting talking about music. I composed a dance to a piece of music and then told my composer that I wanted him to watch my video with no sound and create a song to my dance. He made his piece and then he gave what he made to his wife, who is a musician, and she added a little bit of flute to it. When I put it on my dancers, it was a totally different thing then what I started with. There were all kinds of things happening in the dance that weren't happening anymore with his music. And vice-versa. It's always interesting to collaborate without having the opportunity to change or tweak someone else's aspect of the collaboration. I think that's fun when you think, "This music isn't right for me. Well, this is the music now. Let's go! Annnnnnd showtime!" It was a totally different thing. It wasn't mine. And wasn't his. Suddenly, nobody owned it. It was a thing of its own, that probably neither of us were perfectly satisfied with, but maybe somebody out there thought, "Oh, finally someone understands me." I mean, I don't know. The forced collaborations that you can't fix. Interesting.

Jenny: Sandra, I know that you've also worked with live musicians in some of the black box performances. Can you talk about your relationship with live music and how that worked?

Sandra: Yes. In my experience, the majority of the musicians send you a recording before. That way you can say, "Okay, this is what is happening." This means that we can work with what they want and adapt to their needs. Sometimes we also have a singer from the opera collaborating with us too. So, there are these three elements: the singer, the musicians, and the dancers. So, in this situation, I choreograph to what was sent to me. So, I listen to music, go to the studio, and make the piece. One time, it was 12 o'clock in the night and the conductor said, "By the way, we changed the music." Are you kidding me? I already finished the dance! I didn't say that to him, but I was thinking, "Oh, crap." That means I must change to the new piece

170   A CONVERSATION AMONG ARTISTS

of music. So, I tried to fit the same choreography with the new music. The movement changed completely. It was the same steps. What changed was the way that they worked inside of the score. These types of experiences mean you need to adjust. I actually really enjoy this. I also work often with the musicians who play improvisationally. They create music for us, and we create choreography for them. I really enjoy it because there are moments when I need to give up what I want for movement or sometimes the rhythm they want gives way to the needs of the dance, or I create intention that is different from what the musicians are putting in the movement. Then there were the times that they were feeling inspired by the way I was moving, and then they create for me. I like it. It was very interesting. I really like working with live music because you are feeding off of the energy of the musicians, dancers and music at the same time.

Jenny: What can you all tell me about your style? The three of you choreograph in very different styles. You have different training, vocabularies, and different ways of executing movement. How do you all describe what you make?

Sandra: For me, I guess I need to choreograph different things. I choreograph, of course, Latin and Salsa. The movements are already there so the only thing you're doing is mixing and matching the steps in different counts. For me, you know, that is very easy. It's easy because you repeat the steps over and over. I can put a salsa together tomorrow. When I need to choreograph a ballet piece, I feel like it is easy too, because you do have a vocabulary. Even if it's your own choreography, it's similar movements that you mix and match. And, of course, this needs to be working well with the music. As for the more classical pieces, if you need to recreate a piece or stage a ballet like Don Quixote or something, yes, it is your choreography, but the majority of the phrases and everything are there, and you put your signature on it, and make changes to the movements. They are slight, small changes. I feel like that is okay. When I choreograph my own movement, I choreograph a lot in opposition to what was my training, strangely. Because in the ballet movement, you need to have that arm in this way, the eye in that way, the leg in one specific position, your arm can't be an inch beyond your shoulder. And I like it. It was my life for many years. But that is why the movement of my style is changing completely. I say, "No, don't

A CONVERSATION AMONG ARTISTS   171

hold the arms. Throw your arms and let it go when you pirouette." I feel like it's a way to express the freedom. I like to feel in that moment. It is not any position of the arms in particular. No, I want the arms to go wherever they want. I like to express freedom of the movement. I enjoy dancing contemporary pieces because of the freedom I have to express what I feel versus, needing to look like a beautiful princess or a witch or something. I am respectful of that way of dancing, but my style is, if I have to call it one name, is freedom. I try to feel free in the way that I move.

Liza: That's interesting. I feel like when you're choreographing, and I learn a piece from you, there is a flowing three-dimensional ribbon of movement. I feel like freedom is a really good word for what you're doing because I'm not held in place in space. My energy is allowed to flow. Freedom is a good explanation of yours. ShaLeigh described my work once by saying "Oh, I knew it was Liza's choreography. It's like a rock and roll carnival." I never thought of myself as "rock and roll carnival" but I thought that was cool. My style of movement is a blend of jazz and modern. But I think I've got a little … unloveliness. I'm very purposefully unlovely. I think there's a violence, a bound violence to my movement, and I know that violence isn't a real positive word. It's like breaking things down. I feel the most natural and free when it's a little violent. Well, I don't want to just say bound, because that's just too ….

ShaLeigh: I would say rebellious. There's rebellion. There's something about rebellion, and the expression comes from bumping up against something.

Liza: Yeah, that's a good way to say it! Yes, I'm bumping and I'm breaking through sort of at the same time, and I'm not caring if you find that attractive.

ShaLeigh: I think it's so funny, I just love that we've all worked together so long that we can talk about each other's work. It's so exciting. I feel like the closest I could get to any kind of aesthetic that I have … because it does change depending on the dancers that I'm working with … I feel like it can be more visible and sometimes a little less visible. I really love movement quality more than movement itself, and textures that bodies can create from things that are delicate to powerful to explosive to emotional to purely physical. I feel like the thread that kind of pulls it all together would probably be the broad term of "dance theater" because I feel like there's as much theater as there is movement. And text has always made it into the work, whether it ends up being a source of the inspiration, or it ends up that we've got actors in our work also. So, we don't necessarily tell stories, but I feel like we enter into moments in time of story. I love things that are more purely expressive rather than narrative. I feel like the composition becomes very interesting to me in terms of how you create a sense of emotional time rather than linear time. So, theater's definitely a big part of it even if we drop into an environment and we let something emerge from that environment. I like the layers of experience and challenge and hardship and desire and dream and fantasy and the coexistence of the light and the dark. I feel like I feel like my work tends to almost always have some darkness to it.

Sandra: I need to do a lot of ballet work this June because of the school and having performance opportunities for little dancers. I say "We're going to do Snow White!" and then one of the parents asked me, "Oh, great, what version?" I say "We're going dark. We are going to have blackbirds." What are they called? Crows! "I gonna put dark crows flying with black tutus and feathers everywhere and makeup." But then I remembered, "Oh, crap, this is a kid's ballet!" Yes, of course, I have the cute butterflies and all of this stuff but, when I need to create the characters, my first character was the dark forest. That is the part I cannot wait to create! I like to go dark, too. Yes, of course, I'm going to put the babies as the little butterflies and daisies and I'm going to have the cute costumes and things like that, but that is a completely different scenario. (laughs)

Jenny: Sandra, if you make a dance for the children that are fireflies. Here is advice from many, many years ago: don't get artsy and turn off the lights part way through the dance so the audience sees the lights darting around the stage. (laughs)

Sandra: Yes, you turned the lights off and we didn't see the kids. (laughs)

Jenny: Their parents were not pleased. "All this year, I paid all this money for dance lessons. I just want to see my kid dance and you turned off the lights."

A CONVERSATION AMONG ARTISTS   173

Liza: It was *so* cool!

Jenny: It was so cool! Art verses parents. I guess that's a good lesson. Know your audience. (laughs)

Jenny: Can you all talk about one piece that you made that is your favorite and why you love it?

Sandra: One of the pieces I like the most is one that I made actually recently, when we did music live with the violin and piano. This piece was from Vivaldi. The section that they chose was, music-wise, extremely complicated. Everybody was saying they didn't want that piece because the music was complex, but I said, "Okay, give the music to me." The choreography, turned out very well. I cannot explain why it ended better than my other work. The only explanation can be that that specific time and that moment in my life, I was kind of breathing after so many storms. I was kind of, personally, finally okay. It was sunny again. I don't know if it's related to how I was feeling in that time or because I was doing meditation or just that all the elements were together in the right time in the right moment, and I had the right dancers. It was my favorite because I put in the choreography what I was feeling, going through the storm, and finally coming out. And like Liza said, I didn't care if the people understood what it was. At the start of the piece, I put the dancers just on the ground without the violin and they were just making the sounds of the rain. There were a lot of dancers on the ground making music just with their fingers. And the fusion of the dancer coming out and the music beginning in that moment, and all the movement to come, I don't know, I still feeling like that was my best piece because of the movement and the music and what I want to say.

Liza: It's hard for me because, I don't know what's wrong with me, but I really fall in love with everything I do. (laughs) It's not an artistically smart thing to do, I think. (laughs) But watching this one particular piece really moved me. It was about quantum mechanics. And it was about freaky motion at a distance. It was about black holes, matter, and anti-matter, which seems like a very cold, scientific thing, but it thrills me. I cried because of this dance about quantum mechanics and space. (laughs) It was especially exciting when anti-matter and matter came together. I had a lot of vibratory movement; they're coming at each other and they're about to touch ... they're about to touch ... they're about to touch ... and they instantly destroy one another. And it was perfect and beautiful that everything came together exactly right; the music I chose, the dancers who I chose; they understood what the heck I was trying to do. I'm creating a piece right now in honor of my father, and I have an interesting relationship with my father. It's very loving. We're a very loving family but definitely he is a strong father and a strong force in my life. He wasn't always like, "Oh, sweetie, I'm encouraging you. I'm proud of you." He wasn't always that but, overall, took very good care of us and did his best. He's great guy. He didn't kill me when I was younger which I can't believe thinking back on it. (laughs) I studied him and his favorite things. So, this entire dance is his favorite things. I took them all and mashed them up and then threw them all around space and then felt them. And I showed it to him and he was like, "It's beautiful." He saw golfing. He saw the tennis. I don't know how he saw that, because we took the golfing and destroyed it, and transported it to a point where I don't know how you would know that was golfing. He's like, "Oh, you really saw me." And that was a human piece, which is not necessarily my favorite thing to do. And there was a sister fight in it where the little sister is trying to copy the big sister and then the big sister is like, "Go away." And my brother died in the piece. None of this is explained, and if you watched it, I don't think you'd see anybody die. There were so many moments that, because of my shared experience with my father, this was one piece for one person to really get, and he really got it. I don't usually work like that though. It was unusual. I'd have to say that the galaxy anti-matter quantum mechanics black hole stuff was my favorite piece and more like what I usually make. I can't remember the name right now.

Jenny: Email me the name if you remember. (Editor's note: She did! It was called *Spooky Action at a Distance*)

ShaLeigh: I'll just quickly say that I feel like the piece that I made in New York, *Dedicated To [] Because Of [] (and vice versa)*, was probably one of my favorite pieces because that was me expressing myself. And that's probably the most vulnerable I've ever been with my work and ever given myself permission to dive into. And then the piece that I made in 2019, *The In-Between*, is one of my favorite pieces, one, because I went into a residency and actually had time to develop some material, but two, I had two company members who were able to teach the kind of movement that we played with and their ability to move the way I always envisioned my dancers moving. They nailed it. So, it was the first time I had dancers that could actually do what I wanted to do. The composers that we found for that work was a dream team. It was probably the most seamless composer relationship I've ever had. I feel like I could just take a deep breath, and they'd be like, "Oh, I got it." Everything that they brought in just elevated what we had done. So, that was just a really incredible collaboration of the way things all came together. The costume designer blew it out of the park. So, it was just in a great team and a lot of artistry coming together. So, that was really satisfying. But I would say in my work as a whole, I still have that annoying feeling, and I'm a little bit opposite of Liza in this way, I'm not sure if I'm in love with anything that I've ever done. I have this feeling like I've never made the piece, and I hope I get even a moment of that before I perish. Maybe that's the answer, now that we're going back to the first question, "Why do you do this?" Because I haven't done it yet! Maybe that's how I actually feel because I just I haven't gotten there yet.

Sandra: Maybe, in some moment, I was thinking that I'm too judgmental to myself, because when I see the work of somebody else, I can see the beauty on of it. The majority of the time, even when I was dancing, I was extremely judgmental to myself. I can count a few times during my career of dancing where I felt I was fully dancing great. The majority of the time, I was always looking at what didn't work. And choreography-wise is the same. I always looking at it negatively and I judge myself too much. I don't know if this is a good thing or a bad thing. But I don't like a lot of what I do. And I'm feeling like I cannot have an idea without putting this pressure on myself. I don't have the luxury of being available to choreograph in the moment that I'm feeling inspired. Sometimes, I need to produce pieces one after another, and that is what I call the fabric of dreams. Because you need to get inspired and be creative right now. The problem is I am judging myself too much.

Jenny: I think that so much of being a choreographer is being an editor. Play directors have dramaturges and we don't really have that opportunity so much. So, I think there are so many roles bound up within choreography. I think we have to be creator, director, dramaturge and editor plus rehearsal director, stager and company manager. All three of you all have set work on my students, so I'm going to tell you each my favorite work that you've set. ShaLeigh, the Fibonacci piece that you set was amazing. It was raw and demanding. I loved that it pushed the dancers so hard into directions that were uncomfortable. You challenged them to not only try a new way of moving but you immersed them in a new way of creating. Sandra, my favorite piece of yours is the piece with the 40-foot by 40-foot piece of translucent fabric that reached from offstage left to offstage right and covered one tiny dancer at center stage. She danced under it and then came through it. It was ethereal, graceful, and mesmerizing. The photographs of that dance are like artworks in and of themselves. Liza, my favorite piece of yours, and this is crazy because you've set so many and I think this may be the first one that you ever set but do you remember the one with the blow-up balls that had smiley faces on them? You dressed the dancers in what looked like couture fashion and they looked so bored as they moved and then you introduced these bright, yellow, smiley-faced balloon balls that the dancers threw out into the audience. And, for a while, the audience became part of the dance as they tossed the balls around, concert style. It was incredible and hilarious. You challenged the dancers with acting. Satire in dance is so hard and you nailed it. Thank you all so much. I'm sure we could talk about this for two more hours and I wish we could but then I'd need a second volume of this book (laughs). I want to thank you all so much for such honestly in your craft, for sharing your gifts, and helping to make our world a more beautiful and thoughtful place. Thank you for challenging audiences, teaching young dancers, and loving and contributing to our field. Thank you for all of the zillions of hours of time and effort you've dedicated to collaborating with me and for bravely taking on numerous projects simply because I asked you— including this one. Love you all.

INDEX

Note: Page numbers in *italics* refer to figures in the text.

Acquiescence 15, 17, 20, 22, 29, 30, 43

advice 147–152; "circle back and start something new" 152; "do something with the something" 150; "edit the something" 151–152; "have fun with the something" 152; "keep making something" 151; "record the something" 150–151; "show your something" 152; "start with something" 148–150

aerial dance *105*, 106–107

aesthetics 10, 13, 51–52, 165

agape 25, 30

American Society of Composers, Authors, and Publishers (ASCAP) 139, 140

Angelico, F. 24

"Annunciation" (Howe) 17, 23–24, 27

art 28, 52; definition of 51; entertainment and 53; inspiration dance 66–67; Renaissance 44; visual 23, 67, 152; women in 24

asymmetrical stages 94; *see also* symmetrical stages

"*At Last*" (James) 32, 42

August & September 120, 121–124

authentic movement 58–77; art inspiration dance 66–67; chance dance 69–70; cut-outs dance 62–64; digital media as a tool for 71–77; hand dance 61; hidden camera dance 64–65; improv dance 68–69; motion capture dance 67; prop dance 65; rules dance 62; web dance 68

"Ave Maria" 18, 23, 30

balanced stage 95–96

Ballerini, K.: "Miss Me More" 145

INDEX

Bartenieff, I. 86
beauty 16, 23, 51–52
The Beauty Project 14
Berry, C.: "Johnny B Goode" 27, 31
Beyoncé: "Run the World (Girls)" 145; "Single Ladies (Put A Ring On It)" 145
Blame Game 113, *113*, 114–117
body 52
bodystories 12
Breathing Lessons 110, *111–112*, 112–114
"Brechtian punk cabaret" style music 18
Broadcast Music Incorporated (BMI) 139
Brown, R.: "Oh What A Dream" 27, 31, 37–38
Bruised *132*
the B-side *21*, 22–34, 43–44

Cage, J. 70
canon 30, 90, 91, 96
Cathexis (Dotterer) 153
chance dance 69–70
"Chances Are" (Mathis) 30, 31, 38
"A Change Is Gonna Come" (Cooke and Redding) 105
choreograph 6, 98, 142, 148, 160, 166–168, 170, 175
choreographers 4, 6, 12, 18–19, 22, 53; communication skills 101; composition books for 79; experienced 133; inexperienced 133; use of improvisation 128
choreographic flowchart 78–131, *126*; aerial dance 105, 106–107; alternative 127–131, *129*; *August & September 120*, 121–124; Breathing Lessons *111–112*, 112–114; *The Conversation 119*, 120–121; costumes 104;

Cruel Beauty *103*, 104–106; development 86–89; inspiration 82–83; integration 97–99; ... in these cases, a few seconds of pause *118*, *119–120*; La Fenêtre *122–123*, *124–125*; lighting 114–117; media 121–124; m(other) *108–109*, 110, 112; production 100–103; research 84, 84–85; set 107–110; stimulus 81–82; structure 85; theme 85–86; toolbox 89–97, 99; *The Tragedy of the Commons 125*, 125–127; *Veil of Ignorance 115–116*, 117–118
choreography 8–9, 17, 19, 22, 44, 73, 80, 92, 104–105, 173, 176; concert dance 8; development of 9; idea in 110; musical theater 8; music and 18; students 8, 133; video of 143
Choreography and the Specific Image (Nagrin) 54
Christensen, J. 27
Cole, N. K.: "Mona Lisa" 32
Collage, Tree for Mine (Reed) 66
Collier, J. 23–24
"Come Go With Me" (Del Vikings) 36
communication 52
composition 52; authentic movement 60; dance 28, 76, 79; flowchart 79; taught to students 3, 71
Conceptual Dubstep Song 61
concert dance 8, 54
contrast 96
The Conversation 119, *119*, 120–121
Cooke, S.: "A Change Is Gonna Come" 105
costumes 43, 104, 106–107; design 35, 48, 106, 114, 165; physicality of 104
creativity 25, 50, 52, 64, 79, 102

INDEX   179

critical response process (Lerman) 54, 61, 102–103
Cruel Beauty *103*, 104–106
Cunningham, M. 70
cut-outs dance 62–64

dance-as-art 53, 54
dance-as-entertainment 53, 54
Dance Composition: A Practical Guide to Creative Success in Dance Making (Smith-Autard) 81
DanceForms2 73
Dancemaker 72, 73
dance notator 6
Danzig, E.: *Rhythm I 153*
Davies, Antony 124–125
de Keersmaeker, A. T.: *Rosas Danst Rosas* 145
DEL Dancemaker app 73–74
Del Vikings: "Come Go With Me" 36
development 86–89; body 86; effort 87, 87–88; shape 88; space 88
digital media as tool for authentic movement 71–77
Dotterer, S.: *Cathexis* 153
Dresden Dolls: "Missed Me" 18

Echad Mi Yodea (Naharin) 145
Effort/Shape (Laban theory) 54
"Efforts of Action Drive" (Laban) 87
Elements (editing software) 71
Elkin, D.: *M(oor)town Redux* 25
Emadian, E. R.: *MASCCHAOS* 153
"Era Più Calmo?" 18
eros 25, 31, 42
Evans, S. P. 41, 120–121; *Veil of Ignorance* 95, *115–116*, 116, 117–118
experiencing 5, 20, 168

facings, contrasts in 94
female choreographer 10; *see also* choreographers

feminism 11, 23
Final Cut Pro (editing software) 71
Fleming, R. 18
flexibility in dancing 11, 17
flowchart 78–131; *see also* choreographic flowchart
Fosse, B.: *Mexican Breakfast* 145
fresco 23
"Full Effort Actions" 88

GarageBand 134
Graham, M.: *Lamentations* 54
grand rights 140, 143

hand dance 61
Harptones 30
Helnwein, G.: *Modern Annunciation* 29
hidden camera dance 64–65
Howe, M. 23; "Annunciation" 17, 23–24, 30
Humphrey, D. 39

If I Give My Heart to You 42
iMovie (editing software) 68–69, 71–72, 73, 130
improv dance 68–69
influence of music 133
inspiration: abstract 83; clear 83; literal 83; representational 83; symbolic 83
Instagram 56
integration 97–99
Integrative and Quantitative Center 74–75
intellectual property 138–146; movement 144–146; music 139–144
intent 52, 133
... in these cases, a few seconds of pause 117, *118*, 119–120
In the Still of the Night 28, 38

INDEX

James, E. 32; *"At Last"* 32, 42
"Johnny B Goode" (Berry) 27, 31
Judson Dance Theatre 47–48

King, M. L.: "I Have a Dream" 136
King Tutt 61
Koi in a Storm (Koleva) 153
Koleva, I.: *Koi in a Storm* 153

Laban, R. 86; "Efforts of Action
 Drive" 87
Laban/Bartenieff Movement
 Analysis 80
Laban Movement Analysis 73–74
Laban Movement Analysis/
 Bartenieff Fundamentals
 (LMA/BF) 86
La Fenêtre *122–123*, *124–125*, 155
Lamentations (Graham) 54
Lerman, L.: critical response
 process 54, 61, 102–103
levels, contrasts in 94
Library of Congress 140
lighting 114–117; *see also* costumes

MASCCHAOS (Emadian) 153
Mathis, J.: "Chances Are" 30, 31, 38
McIntyre, T.: *Mercury Half Life* 25
media 121–124
Medieval 23
Mercury Half Life (McIntyre) 25
Mexican Breakfast (Fosse) 145
Michelangelo 28
Miller, J. 106
misogyny 28
"Missed Me" (Dresden Dolls) 18
"Miss Me More" (Ballerini) 145
Modern Annunciation (Helnwein) 29
modern dance 10, 11
modern dancers 13
"Mona Lisa" (Cole) 32
M(oor)town Redux (Elkin) 25

m(other) *36, 40, 41, 44, 78,
 108–109,* 110–112
motherhood 20, 45
mothering 11, 20, 23
motion capture: in dance 67, 75–77;
 of student dancer 71
movement 52; intellectual property
 144–146; *see also* authentic
 movement
music 132–137; choreography and
 18; influence of 133; intellectual
 property 139–144; issues faced
 by choreographers 135; purpose
 of 135; rights 139; score 136
musical theater choreography 8
Music Publishers Association
 (MPA) 139

Nagrin, D.: *Choreography and the
 Specific Image* 54; "'Rules' for
 Choreography" 54
Naharin, O.: *Echad Mi Yodea* 145
naming game 98
negative space 94
92Y Dance Education Library 72
92Y Harkness Dance Center 72
not dance 46, 46–48

"Oh What A Dream" (Brown) 27, 31,
 37–38
"Only You" (Platters) 38
orientation 6, 63
Otello (Verdi) 18, 23
out of unison 94

painting 3–4, 24, 29, 39, 66–67,
 83–84
performing artists 81
personal rules 95
Pfaff, D. 74, 75
philos 25, 28, 38
"Piangea Cantando" 18

Platters: "Only You" 38
Primus, Pearl: *Strange Fruit* 136
process 7–45; the 25th of March 35–45; acquiescence 20–22; the B-side *21, 22–34*
production 100–103
professional dancers 12, 14
prop dance 65

Redding, O.: "A Change Is Gonna Come" 105
Reed, R. J.: *Collage, Tree for Mine* 66
refinement 79, 84, 89, 107
Renaissance 23
research 84–85; triangle *84*
reverse engineering 8
rewinding-canon 96
Rhythm I (Danzig) *153*
Roman Catholic Marian 23
Rosas Danst Rosas (de Keersmaeker) 145
rules dance 62
"'Rules' for Choreography" (Nagrin) 54
"Run the World (Girls)" (Beyoncé) 145

score 136
selection 84, 89
set 107–110
shapemaking 6, 16, 18
Shout 41, 42
"Single Ladies (Put A Ring On It)" (Beyoncé) 145
Smith-Autard, J.: *Dance Composition: A Practical Guide to Creative Success in Dance Making* 81
social media 55–57
Society of European Stage Authors and Composers (SESAC) 139
So You Think You Can Dance 130

stage balance 6
"Stay" (Zodiacs and Williams) 39
steps 128, 130
stimulus 81–82
Stoiser, L.: *Untitled 153*
Strange Fruit (Primus) 136
structure 85; class 48; linear 3; tools of external 89, 94, 97; tools of internal 89, 91, 97; vocabulary and 74
student dancer *58, 147*; 3D printing of *74, 76*; motion capture of *71*
"A Sunday Kind of Love" 30, 38
symmetrical stages 94; *see also* asymmetrical stages

Tanner, H. O. 24, 32
Taubman Museum of Art in Roanoke, Virginia 21
theme 85–86
This is a dance? 48
This Macaroni and Cheese Crayon Tastes Like Wax, 138
3D printing of student dancer *74, 76*
TikTok 68
toolbox 89–97, 99
tools of external structure 89, 94–97
tools of internal structure 89–94, 97
The Tragedy of the Commons 124, *125*, 125–127
transitions 94
trial 84
The 25th of March 34, 35–45
Twitter 56

unison 94
United Parcel Service (UPS) 26, 28–29, 31–33, 35–36, 40, 43, 45
Untitled (Stoiser) *153*
US Copyright Office 140

INDEX

van Wissen, S. 145
Veil of Ignorance (Evans) 95, *115*, *116*, *117*–118
Verdi: *Otello* 18, 23
videoing assignments 60
virtual reality (VR) 76
visual artists 81; *see also* art
vocabulary 49–57; social media and 55–57

Wall Flowers/Wild Flowers *143*
web dance 68, 146

Williams, M.: "Stay" 39
women 18, 29, 53; independent artists 13; inequality of 25; innate power of 16; modern dance 10; suffering and demoralizing of 6, 27; weighty issues 17
World of Dance 130

Zodiacs: "Stay" 39